Generations

A South Asian Seniors
Cookbook for Canadian Youth

Generations: A South Asian Seniors Cookbook for Canadian Youth

Copyright © 2012 Aangan

Give feedback on the book at:
aanganquebec@gmail.com

Printed in Canada
ISBN 978-1479186303

Acknowledgement

This project was conceived by the CENTRE DE BIEN-ETRE FAMILLES D'ORGINE SUD-ASIATIQUE AANGAN INC. This project (#10319713) was supported through a grant from Services Canada under their "New Horizons for Seniors Program". We,the Executives of Aangan greatly appreciate the support received from Services Canada. This project would not have been possible without their support. Publication of this cook book achieves the objectives we set out to meet in our grant application.This project directly supports the priority established by Quebec by enabling seniors to maintain their personal skills while facilitating the transfer of their knowledge and wisdom to the next generation youth.

We are thankful to all the seniors, youth and volunteers who so enthusiatically participated in this project.

Ranjana Jha
President

Sudershan Bhatla
Vice President

Gurjeet Sehmi
Treasurer

Monisha Poonia
Secretary

A Cookbook Revealed
From our elders to you

The wealth of our senior's culinary talents is available in abundance;
The archives of their minds hold the flavors and aromas of yesteryears

Having travelled a passage of time, displaced from their native homes and resettlement they maintain their self-identity in habits and foods, crystalized by memories from their youth and flavors from kitchens long gone.

These memories and recipes have long been kept in their heart, until today.

The desire to relive these tastes is awakened.
Generations to come will be enriched today

Today's youth is in want of learning, treasured recipes and tips outweigh any food fads. The recipes in these pages appeal to our soul– many are the foods of ancestors. Our aim is to enrich the lives of today's youth with recipes of the past and hopefully for their future.

This beautiful dream of capturing timeless memories in the form of a cookbook was converted into a reality and made possible with the support of The Government of Canada New Horizons for Seniors program.

Gratitude and Thanks

Our cookbook would have been an impossible dream without the many hands that joined together in making it a reality. To all those who stirred pots, recounted journeys through food and those who listened with open ears, a big Thank You! The volunteers who car-pooled, phone called, gathered recipes, purchased supplies and transcribed recipes are the invisible hands behind the making of this cookbook. To all the members of Aangan, its Board and its volunteers, we extend our heart-filled thanks.

Our immense gratitude of thanks to Maral Verma, Monisha Poonia, Nisha Catherine Sharma, Malika Verma Kashyap, Vir Kashyap, Paras Khare, Parul Khare, Rupali Chaudhri, Karine Sirois, Claire Acoca, Shalini Jha, Sapna Mahawal, Amelia Mounsey, Claire Raymond Sharma, Nini Singh, Ryan Szawlowski, Francis Ward, Devansh Srivastava, Karel Painchaud, Ashish Jain, Rina Sehmi, Roohi Saeed, Gurjeet Sehmi, Kamla Bir, Sudarshan Bhatla, Michel Bayard, Dishya Semhi, Pooja Kaushal and the contributing persons who wished to remain anonymous.

During the course of making this book, most unfortunately, we witnessed the departure of three of our dear seniors.

Bahadur Bhatla was our Vice-President and had been the past Principal of St-Georges School. He also had a keen eye and would have been incredibly involved in the making of this book, combing through it finely. His knowledge and guidance are largely missed.

Lila Vati Sharma was very visible in our community. She was well known for her beautiful garden, freshly grown vegetables and renowned for her cooking. Her generosity and advice to many was really appreciated. She was seen driving and cooking into her late 80's. She is dearly missed.

Devinder Dev Kaushal, a retired engineer, was truly a remarkable gentleman. He turned out to be a master chef and cooked right into his 90's. He succeeded in his creation of taking traditional Indian recipes and perfecting them with the use of a microwave. Out of all our seniors interviewed for this cookbook, he is the only one who has left behind his own hand written cookbook. His playfulness, funny comments and positive attitude in life are greatly missed by family and friends.

We appreciate and thank Vito Vittoria of Les fruitières Vittoria Inc. and Samar Indian Food Store for contributing and subsidizing products for the cookbook.

Our deepest gratitude to the Government of Canada, New Horizon for Seniors Program. We thank them for understanding this project and the need for our organization to create this unique cookbook. We profoundly thank them for making it possible and allowing us to revisit Southeast Asian food culture to benefit our youth and give joy to our seniors to impart their knowledge.

We do appreciate your understanding that any grammatical errors and omissions are not intentional, please overlook if any. We hope you enjoy reading this book as much as we enjoyed putting it together.

Aangan
Centre du bien-etre des familles d'origine
sud-asiatique

Nalini Chaudhri Verma
Coordinator
CENTRE DE BIEN-ETRE FAMILLES D'ORGINE SUD-ASIATIQUE AANGAN INC.

Nutritional Facts for Balanced Meals

Dr. Kamala Bir spoke at an Aangan gathering for seniors and youth. The event consisted of food tastings and story sharing. With her background in bio-chemistry and as a nutritionist, plus her wisdom over the years, she explained that we need food for two reasons:

1) When we are young- to grow
2) When we age- to maintain a healthy body

In simple and easy to understand language, she stressed these facts for balanced meals and nutrition. Our foods must contain proteins, carbohydrate, fats, vitamins and minerals with trace elements, as well as water. Her voice left a positive impact to pay heed to why and what we were eating ...and what it was really doing to our bodies.

Proteins

Proteins are part of every cell in the human body and are either complete or incomplete. Of the 22 amino acids, eight are considered essential. She explained a complete protein is a source for all eight essential amino acids; or in simple terms, the building blocks for the body tissue.

Most animal based foods contain a complete protein. Meat, fish, milk, eggs and cheese are examples. She mentioned that eggs are a complete protein and cook easily. Quinoa is a rare example of a vegetable source of complete protein. We offered our Quinoa Kheer as a sample and it was well reviewed and got positive feedback on texture, taste and was an eye opener for its many benefits. It is not a common ingredient amongst the South Asian community, however was praised by all who attended the event.

Most vegetable sources of protein are incomplete, which means they lack one or more of the essential amino acids. She explained that this could be easily remedied by eating common foods in pairs. For example, rice and beans, bread and peanut butter, or milk and cereal are possible combinations to make an incomplete protein into a complete form. The recommended daily intake by the US department of Agriculture is 0.4 grams per pound of the ideal body weight. Overconsumption of protein is hard for the liver and kidneys. Moderation is always key to a healthy diet.

Carbohydrates

Carbohydrates are the most important source of energy for the body. They are either simple or complex depending on their chemical structure. They are the organic compounds that consist of carbon, hydrogen and oxygen. Simple carbohydrates include sugars found naturally in foods such as fruits, vegetables, milk or in refined sugars. Complex carbohydrates take longer to breakdown into glucose. They include starch naturally found in grains, cereals, starchy vegetables and are a good source of fiber. By going on a diet or cutting down on carbohydrates, the body becomes stressed trying to convert the protein into carbohydrates. The body uses carbohydrates to make glucose which is the fuel that gives the body energy and helps keep everything going. Glucose can be used immediately by the body or stored in the liver and muscles until needed. One has to be careful about foods higher in carbohydrates such as sodas and candies that have added sugars, are high in calories and lack nutrients.

Calories

A calorie is a unit of measurement. It is the energy needed to raise the temperature of 1 gram of water by 1 degree Celsius. This demonstrates how our body transforms energy from the calories you eat and drink. Eating too many calories and not burning enough of them through activities can lead to weight gain, thus the reasoning for their bad reputation. In every gram of carbohydrates and protein, there are 4 calories; and for every gram of fat, there are 9 calories. In sum, the 'good' carbohydrates have more fiber and complex properties and the 'bad' carbohydrates are more refined and have added sugars (e.g. white flour).

Fats

The word fat makes it sound as if it's something you should not eat and it is bad for you. Dr. Bir was able to clarify the importance of fat in a balanced diet and not to consider them an enemy but rather see which kind is a friend. They help the brain and nervous system develop correctly and help the body absorb nutrients from food.

There are two main types fats, saturated and unsaturated. Both contain the same amount of calories. Essential fatty acids are important as well. 'Good' fats, monounsaturated and polyunsaturated fats, lower disease risks. 'Bad' fats, saturated and especially trans fat, increase disease risk.

Foods high in 'bad' fats included red meats, butter, cheese, ice cream, and processed foods made with trans fat from partially hydrogenated oil. Low fat, reduced fat and fat-free are terms that negatively promote the importance of fat in a healthy diet. One must choose foods that have more good fats than bad. Over time, reducing the minimum required fats from your daily diet and replacing it with carbohydrates can raise the risk of heart disease and diabetes.

Facts about fats are confusing; remember when margarine was supposed to be better than butter? Then we found out it was worse. Fat is an essential part of the diet. Trans fats result when liquid oils are pumped with hydrogen to make them solid. This gives processed foods longer shelf life at the risk of maybe shortening yours by clogging arteries. Goods fats are calorie rich.

1) Butter - saturated fat
2) Hard margarine – trans fat
3) Soft tub margarine – unsaturated fat
4) Vegetable Shortening – trans fat
5) Plant oils (olive, canola, sunflower, corn, soy) – unsaturated fat
6) Tropical oils (palm, palm kernel, coconut) – saturated fat
7) Desi Ghee or Asli Ghee – saturated fat

Carbohydrates, fats and proteins are the three types of fuel our body requires for energy. They mainly come from the foods we consume and are classified as macronutrients. Carbohydrates are the fuel source our bodies use most often. Proteins are made of numerous organic components called amino acids. These acids combine to form lengthy chains called polypeptides that help to break down eaten food during digestion. This process leaves behind the molecules called amino acids. Since fat is notorious for its tendency to accumulate if consumed in excess, it is nevertheless a critical part of a nutritious diet. Fatty acids are made of carbon atoms arranged in different patterns. Fatty acids can be saturated, monounsaturated or polyunsaturated depending on the type of bond linking together certain atoms. Amino acids and fatty acids have two categories, essential and non-essential acids. Our bodies cannot produce essential acids independently so we must obtain it through our diets or supplements. The popular omega-3 and omega-6 are the two essential fatty acids (flaxseed, nuts, fish). Amino acids help the body grow. We cannot produce essential fatty acids because our bodies do not have the enzymes needed to create the required bonds between certain kinds of atoms in some fatty acids. Therefore, what the body cannot produce must be provided in the diet.

Vitamins are either water soluble or fat-soluble organic substances, both essential and required in minute amounts for normal growth and full body activity. Vitamins are naturally found from animal or plant foods. Vitamins aids in maintaining healthy digestion, reduce cancer risk, stop bleeding when wounded, bone health, blood circulation, growth, vision, body healing etc. When we eat food with fat-soluble vitamins, they get stored in the fat tissue of the body and in the liver, for example, vitamin A, D, E and K; and the body uses them as per need.

When we eat food with water-soluble vitamins, they cannot be stored in the body and keep circulating in the blood stream. The body uses a part as per need right away and the rest gets out of the body through the urine, for example vitamin B and its group (B1-2-3-5-6-7-9-12) commonly called vitamin B Complex as well as vitamin C. They are such importance substances that the deficiency of them will interfere with normal metabolic functions.

Micronutrients are subdivided to the quantities needed in the human diet. If more than 100 grams per day of an element is needed, it is classified as mineral. Calcium, sodium, magnesium, phosphorus, sulphur, potassium and chlorine are seven essential minerals and play a very important role to maintain a healthy body. Essential substances really needed daily in amounts of less than 100mg a day are classified as trace elements. Iron, copper, zinc, molybdenum, iodine, magnesium, selenium and chromium are amongst the many other trace elements. In very simple terms, minerals maintain life and are basic components of all matter. Enzymes, cells, bones, blood and body fluids all benefits from them. They aid in all aspects from hormones, energy production, digestion, muscle contraction, body fluid regulation, PH levels, reproduction and muscle tissue. All minerals and trace elements, along with vitamins, are absolutely essential nutrients which function in the body and are critical of how a body grows, develops, functions and performs.

Vitamins consumed need adequate minerals in the body to work well. There are more than 100 minerals and elements on our Earth. Five of these, oxygen, hydrogen, carbon, sulphur and nitrogen, make over approximately 95% of mass and are generally freely available (nitrogen may need to be supplemented). The remaining approximate 5% has all of the other macro minerals.

To conclude, a daily balanced meal is one that comprises all of the foods mentioned here in some form or another. Water is the best drink to help keep the flow in the human system. The building blocks should be available at the same time to assist the body in maintaining good health. This is very important; otherwise, the body will not be able to fully use the maximum benefit of whatever is being eaten.

Dr. Kamla Goyal Bir completed her B.Sc and M.Sc. from Punjab University with honors. After receiving her master's degree in Chemistry in 1958, she went to Purdue University in Indiana, USA to pursue her Phd. In 1963, she began teaching nutrition and bio-chemistry as a professor at Lady Irwin College in New Delhi, India. In 1966 she was acting Dean for Home Science College, Agriculture University in Ludhiana, Punjab.

In 1968, she married Montreal resident Dr. Krishan Bir. At the Montreal General Hospital, Douglas Hospital, Saint-Mary Hospital and Reddy Hospital, Dr. Krishan Bir is known as the one who began the Department for Behavioural Therapy program.

Today as a grandmother, Dr. Kamla Goyal Bir is enjoying her retirement and helps out wherever she can assist.

A few words from Dr. Shalini Jha,

I was very delighted and excited when I first heard that this cookbook was being created. It is wonderful to see our senior population show case their talents. As we grow older the memories and food that we experienced throughout our life become more significant and we often turn to them to find comfort in reliving these moments. The recipes our elderly carry with them are like personal history books that tell the tale of our heritage.

Furthermore, food is one of those few things that can connect both our body and soul. This cookbook is a brilliant way for all of us to appreciate and understand our older generation and, in turn, ourselves.

The most common complaint I receive from my geriatric patients is that they feel isolated and that they no longer have a sense of purpose. I think that this cookbook is a good example of how we can bridge the needs of our youth with those of our seniors. I can just imagine younger Indo-Canadians learning how to cook, while these chef-historians pass on our ancient culture, and all the while enjoying good company and even a few laughs together.

This cookbook is a celebration of food, culture, age and life. I can't wait to taste the dishes these stories create.

Dr Shalini Jha was born and raised in Montreal, she received her medical degree from Royal College of Surgeons, Ireland. She did her internal medicine residency at Fletcher Allen Hospital in Burlington Vermont and is currently pursuing a geriatrics fellowship at the London Health Science Centre.

Table Of Contents

Notable Regional Cuisines

Due to the vast diversity of South Asian cultures, cuisine varies according to the region:

North: Awadhi – Punjabi – Kumauni – Mughlai – Kashmir – Rajasthani –Uttar Pradeshi

Northeast: Assamese – Meghalayan – Manipuri – Naga – Sikkimese – Tripuri– Arunachalese

East: Bengali – Oriya – Bihari – Bhojpuri

West: Pakistani – Goan – Gujarati – Marathi – Malvani & Konkani – Sindhi – Parsi

South: Andhra – Malayali – Tamil – Hyderabadi – Udupi – Mangalorian – Mangalorian Catholic - Saraswat - Chettinad

Other Foods: Indian Chinese – Nepali – Jain – Anglo~Indian – Malaysian Indian Cuisine

Through the process of making this cookbook, Aangan and its volunteers have uncovered the rich culinary diversity of various South Asian regions; gathering recipes from Punjab, Kashmir, Rajasthan, Uttar Pradesh, Uttar Aanchal, Assam, Bengal, Bihar, Pakistan, Goa, Gujarat, Maharashtra, Karnataka, Kerala, Hyderabad and Mangalore.

We have gained insights into Mughlai, Sindhi, Parsi, Tamil, Mangalorian Catholic, Indian-Chinese and Jaini cuisine through individuals who moved to Canada and have adapted their dishes to the local ingredients and taste buds of their children who are born and raised in Canada .They now make unique Indo Canadian foods.

The term 'Indian food' is the sum of different regional cuisines. The common thread throughout is the liberal use of spices. Diversity in cuisine occurs by the local styles associated with provinces or districts.

North and West – use chapatis, rotis with their dals, vegetables and curds. Chutney and achar are in every household. Kashmiri and Mughalai food reflects the strong influence of Central Asia over the course of time. Consumption of milk and its products are very high. People from this region are mainly tea drinkers and in the hot weather prefer to drink Nimbu Pani (fresh lime water) or lassi (yoghurt drink) to cool down.

South and East –Consume large quantities of rice and rice-based breads. Coconut is very important. Fish is a large part of the diet along with dal and curries. In the South, coffee is more in demand and cooling coconut water is popular as well. Desert areas such as Rajasthan and Gujarat lack many fresh vegetables; therefore, consumption of dals, achar and red chilies is high.

All over India, whole wheat, lentils and vegetables are popular. In snacks, samosas, pakoras, vadas, tikkis and chaat are common and most popular.

Traditionally, meals were eaten while sitting on the floor with all family members being served by the ladies of the house, but today chairs are used in most households and everyone eats together. Sitting crossed-legged is believed to increase the blood concentration on the digestive organs. Presently, many of our seniors stay in rural areas or small towns of India to avoid the cold months here in Canada. Some so enjoy sitting on their little cots or charpais outside in the sun and are served food there by family members.

One common habit throughout India is food eaten with the use of fingers. One major factor for this continued habit is the reasoning that hands are cleaner than cutlery. Many seniors also describe eating as a sensual process. The ideal is not to fill the stomach but rather be able to enjoy the eating process with overall joy and use the senses of sight, smell, taste and touch. Food broken by hand is easier to chew and it aids in the digestive process. It is an integrated ritual to wash the hands before and after the meal. One can still commonly see this done in a bowl of warm water and a slice of lemon in most restaurants.

DESSERTS

Recently, an Indian wedding ceremony concluded and its guests were led to lunch. They immediately began to feast their eyes upon the food-laden tables. We could not help but notice how one of our seniors, without hesitation, went straight to the dessert table. She returned smiling, holding a plate of sweets in her hands. Enjoying eating the gaajar ka halwa, her sparkling eyes danced in true delight. Her happy voice told us how on joyous occasions, festivities or at mauraths, she or her elders always began the meal with a sweet dish.

During the process of making this cookbook, this same fact was also heard by the volunteers who gathered the recipes from the seniors. To see one of our seniors serve herself this old-fashioned way gave us the idea to start the recipes with this theme. With this tradition in mind, we offer you the following pages…

Carrot Burfi

Ingredients: (Serves 6)

- 1 cup carrot - grated
- ½ litre milk
- 5 tbsp ghee or unsalted butter
- 1 cup coconut - grated
- 1 cup sugar
- ½ cup cashew nuts - crushed

Method:

1. Separately fry the grated carrot and grated coconut without using oil or ghee, only till liquids are dry
2. Boil the milk with sugar until sugar dissolves. Keep stirring to prevent sticking to bottom.
3. Mix in the carrot and coconut and stir again. Mixture should become thick.
4. When it is cooked well (10min), add cashew nut pieces.
5. Apply ghee on a tray and put the mixture in it. Drizzle chopped nuts on top.
6. Cut it into pieces when cooled and serve.

A very satisfying sweet, this carrot fudge is popular and sold in many food stores today, though it is easy to make at home. Some ladies say they put in melon seed or almonds, and cover with it chandi ka varak (silver).

Quinoa Kheer

Ingredients: (Serves 6)

- 1 litre milk
- 1 ½ cup quinoa
- ½ cup sugar
- 2 tbsp. almonds chopped
- 1 tsp. cardamom powder

Method:

1. Boil quinoa in milk until it thickens
2. Add remaining ingredients and stir well.
3. Cool and enjoy!

Mrs. Sudarshan Bhatla has been living in Canada since the early 60s. She is a retired school teacher who still teaches by example of living life to the fullest. Quinoa contains all the eight-essential amino acids making it a valuable protein resource. It is high in fiber, a complex carbohydrate; it has vitamin E, calcium, iron and other minerals. It is gluten-free and comes in a range of colors, but white or golden seeds are its most common forms. Quinoa is popularly used these days in salads and soups and can be used instead of rice or pasta in dishes.

Meethi Sev

Ingredients: (Serves 12)

- 250 gram packet of sev
- 10 oz. white sugar
- 7 ½ cups water
- 5 tbsp. butter
- 1 tsp. cardamom powder
- ½ tsp. nutmeg powder
- Kesar (pinch)
- ¼ cup finely chopped almonds and/or pistachios

Method:

1. Crush the sev into small pieces (should fit into 3 cups).
2. Melt the butter in a large pot.
3. Add the sev and cook on medium heat until golden brown (stir constantly).
4. Add the water.
5. Cook in medium heat until the water evaporates.
6. Add the sugar.
7. Cook on medium heat until the sugar dries up and becomes a thick syrup.
8. Add cardamom, nutmeg & kesar.
9. Pour the mixture into a large tray (approx. 2 inches deep).
10. Garnish with almonds and/or pistachios and cool.
11. Cut into 2 inch by 2 inch squares and serve.

Mrs. Shardha Pattni has many Gujrati preparations and lives in a joint family structure. She enjoys fussing over her children and grandchildren with special dishes.

Quinoa Kheer

Besan Burfi

Ingredients: (Serves 8)

- 1 cup besan
- 3/4 cup ghee
- 1 cup milk powder
- 1 ½ cup sugar

Method:

1. Melt ghee and fry besan till a nice roasted aroma comes out and it has darkened in color. If the besan is not fully cooked through, it will result in a raw tasting burfi
2. Transfer the mixture in another vessel and mix with the milk powder.
3. Make thick sugar syrup by
4. Add the besan mixture in the sugar syrup and stir it.
5. Transfer it to a greased plate. Let cool.
6. Cut in diamond shaped pieces and serve

A very popular item and made in many households here in Canada, especially on Tuesdays where the seniors make it as a Prasad for their prayers. A few seniors mentioned how they look forward to Tuesdays where they can enjoy a piece of this sweet.

Rasgulla

Ingredients: (Makes 40 Gullas)

- 4L of 3.25% milk
- 2 tsp. cream of wheat
- ½ tsp. cardamom powder
- ¼ cup white vinegar
- 1/2 cup regular water
- Rose water

- **For Syrup:**
- 3 cups sugar
- 6 cups regular water

Method:

1. Boil milk in pot.
2. Separately, boil water and add vinegar once boiled
3. Add vinegar & water into boiled milk. The milk will tear (becoming solid paneer – like soft cheese) and will separate from the water.
4. Strain the paneer into cheese cloth and hang 2 to 3 hours so that water drains. Be careful! Make sure the paneer doesn't over dry.
5. Take down the paneer and knead it.
6. Add cream of wheat to the paneer and mix in well.
7. Make little 1 inch balls out of the mixture and put aside.
8. Make the syrup by dissolving the sugar in water and bring to a boil in a 4L pressure cooker.
9. Turn off heat and add cardamom to syrup.
10. Add 8 balls to the syrup in the pressure cooker at high heat. Wait 5 minutes for a whistle.
11. After one whistle, turn off the pressure cooker and remove from heat.
12. After a few minutes when the cooker is cool, take out the rasgullas and put into another container.
13. Repeat steps 11 to 13 until all balls are cooked.
14. If you feel the syrup is becomes thick, add some water to it in the process.
15. Once rasgullas are made, add the left over syrup from the pressure cooker to the rasgulla dish.
16. Cool down the rasgullas, sprinkle a little bit of rose water and serve.

Asha Khare has been making rasgullas for her family for the last 30 years. This airy and light sweet is very much appreciated by her 3 children.

Boondi Ladoo

Ingredients: (Serves 4-6)

- 1 cup besan
- 1 ½ cup sugar
- 2 cardamoms
- 2 cloves
- 4 cashews
- Pinch of saffron

- Pinch of dry camphor (pachai karpooram)
- Pinch of coloring agent –orange or yellow (if desired)
- Oil – to deep fry
- Chandivarak (decorative silver)

Method:

1. Heat up ¼ cup of water in a heavy-bottomed vessel and dissolve the sugar completely in it with the cloves.
2. Add the cardamom, dry camphor, saffron and coloring agent. Then remove from heat and take out the cloves.
3. In another bowl, add ¼ cup of water to the besan and mix it to obtain a thick batter
4. Heat up oil in a kadai, once it starts to smoke, reduce the heat to medium.
5. Hold a ladle with holes used while frying over the hot oil. The smaller the holes, the smaller the boondi.
6. Pour the besan batter over the ladle. Small drops of it will fall in the hot oil and fry as small balls. Remove this promptly (before it becomes too crisp). You can knock the ladle on the rim of the kadai carefully to get even sized boondis.
7. Drain off the excess oil. Add these in batches to the hot sugar syrup.
8. Cool. Mix in nuts and roll the laddoos. Decorate with chandivarak if desired.

These are the most common Ladoos in India. Some of our Bengali and Gujrati seniors enjoy eating these in yogurt. They are served for spiritual offerings, and eaten during festivities, weddings and auspicious occasions. Even here in Canada, many families still serve these ladoos when giving out wedding invites. The larger the boondi, less is the labor . Hence, the smallest Motichur boondi ladoos are highly sought out!

Barfi

Ingredients: (Serves 8)

- 1 cup sugar
- ½ cup 15% cream
- ¾ cup milk
- ½ lb. unsalted butter
- ¼ to ½ cup of ground almonds
- 1/4 cup pistachios - ground
- 4 1/2 cups milk powder

Method:

1. Mix the first 4 ingredients in a pot and bring them to boil over medium heat.
2. Boil for 2-3 minute (count the minutes from when first boil appears)
3. Remove pot from heat.
4. Add milk powder while stirring slowly the milk mixture.
5. Cook at medium-low heat and stir continuously to avoid lumps.
6. Keep stirring on low heat until mixture turns beige and releases its aroma.
7. Add the ground ilaichi and nuts (optional).
8. Pour this mixture onto a greased tray to set till firm (approximately 2 hours).
9. Cover with chandivarak and cut into diamond shape pieces to serve.

Keep this dish in an air tight container in the fridge. Members suggested getting Raj Kalia to share this barfi recipe with the Aangan group as hers is really good. However, Raj insisted it's not the ingredients, but rather the care and techniques in making a good barfi by feel and proper estimations that makes it perfect. Technique and time given to cook can change the outcome of her barfi. Indeed, a labor of love which has come all the way from India via Africa here to Canada.

Gaajar Halwa

Gaajar Halwa

Ingredients: (Serves 8-10)

- 4 cups grated carrots
- 2 cups whole milk (3%)
- 5 tbsp. ghee
- ½ cup sugar
- 1 tsp. cardamom powder

- 1 cup of 35% cream
- Almonds, cashew and raisins to taste

Method:

1. Boil carrots in milk until they turn soft.
2. In a food processer, coarsely grind the mixture.
3. In a pot, add ghee and ground carrots. Stir.
4. Add sugar and cream and cook until mixture turns thick.
5. Turn the heat off and add the remaining ingredients.

This tasty desert is made by Mrs. Indravati Sharma is mastered by her son Rastra Sharma. It is also known as "Gajrala" in Punjabi and generally can take lots of patience to make. The Sharma household found a way to make this tasty version by grinding the carrots instead of slow-cooking them. In this large joint family household the kitchen is a busy place where amazing foods are prepared from the products grown in their garden and shared by anyone who drops into their home.

Mohanthal

Ingredients: (Serves 12)

- 4 cups besan
- 3 cups ghee or unsalted butter
- 2 cups sugar
- 8 oz. khoya
- 1 tbs. ground cardamom

- ¼ cup almonds

Method:

1. In ghee, brown the besan at medium heat till fragrant.
2. Add khoya and stir continuously for 2-3 min.
3. In another pot, add 1 cup of water and sugar. Bring to boil and simmer to make a 2-thread syrup. To test for doneness – take a bit of syrup in a spoon and press between forefinger and thumb to see if you get 2 strands of sugar.
4. Pour this syrup into besan-khoya mix and on med-low heat stir the sugar syrup with besan-khoya mixture till thick.
5. Add cardamom and almond and then pour onto greased thali until it sets.
6. Cut into square shapes with knife, put whole almond on top of each piece if desired and serve.

Over the years, from East Africa to Canada, Raj Kalia has enjoyed making this dessert. A real treat for the palate, Mohanthal is easy to prepare and a favorite during festivities and auspicious occasions.

Gulab Jamun

Ingredients: (Makes 30 Jammuns)

- 2 cups (16 ounces) Carnation milk
- 1\2 cup all purpose flour
- 1\4 tsp baking powder
- 250 ml whipping cream
- 2 cups white sugar
- 2 cups cold water
- 1 liter of cooking oil

Method:

1. Dissolve the sugar in water and bring to a boil. Turn off heat.
2. Mix the rest of ingredients and knead gently till you start feeling the oil on the palms of your hands.
3. Roll the dough into small size balls.
4. Fry the balls on medium heat till they are brown.
5. Drain the balls on a paper towel and keep aside.
6. When ready place the balls individually in the syrup.
7. Turn on the heat until syrup starts to boil, then turn it off and let it cool.
8. Serve it hot or cold.

Like many others who migrated to Canada Nighat Khan recalls how in the seventies here in Montreal, many ideas and suggestions and lengthy discussions would take place amongst the ladies to get a real good soft tasty gulab jamun. Real khoya was impossible to find then and today she has mastered this recipe – enjoying many fond memories related to it. An amazing cook we could write a whole cookbook of her recipes.

Bread Ladoo

Ingredients: (Makes 12)

- 10 slices of bread
- ¼ cup powdered sugar
- 5 tsp ghee
- 5 cashews
- 5 small almonds – crushed
- 3 cardamoms – crushed or powder

Method:

1. Remove the crust from the breads.
2. Put the bread in the mixer/food processor or break finely by hand to get coarse crumbs. Put in bowl.
3. Add powdered sugar and cardamom powder to the bread. Mix well.
4. In a frying pan, heat ghee. Fry the cashews and almonds.
5. Add nuts and ghee mixture to bread mix. Roll small balls. Adjust ghee to be able to roll the laddu.

After the British Sarker rule in India, bread began to be commonly available. Some seniors recall this fast laddu emerged in the village, to use up stale bread. A bread halva became very popular as well, by roasting the bread in ghee until smooth and red and adding sugar and nuts. The fusion and creativity began to
emerge in Indian households and still continues .Sitaji makes this as a halwa by adding milk to the recipe to serve it for breakfast.

Methi Ladoos

Ingredients: (Makes 12)

- 1 ¼ cup wheat flour
- 1 ¼ cup almonds – crushed
- 1 ¼ cup fenugreek seeds – grounded
- 1 ¼ cup dry coconut
- 4 tbsp coriander seeds – crushed
- ½ cup gond (edible gum)

- 3 tsps dried ginger powder
- 1 tsp – cardamom – powder
- 2 ½ cup gur (jaggery)
- Ghee for frying

Method:

1. Heat ghee in a large frying pan. Fry gond until it puffs and remove from ghee, then cool and grind finely.
2. In same pot, add flour, and stir-fry on low heat for several minutes.
3. Stir continuously, adding about one tbsp of ghee
4. Add almonds, fenugreek, coconut, coriander, ginger and cardamom into flour mixture.
5. Add more ghee if flour becomes very dry.
6. In a separate pan, heat another cup or so of ghee and the jaggery, melt while stirring continuously.
7. Allow little bubbles to form but do not overcook or the ladoos will become hard.
8. Mix this into the rest of the mixture and gond. With a wide strong spatula, stir mixture to mix well and hand roll ladoos.
9. Store in airtight container

Some believe 'Methi, menthis, fenugreek' help in preventing joint aches and pains. This is a popular dessert for seniors for medicinal purposes and given to young athletes as well. Seniors mentioned how they feel that they should have started eating this when they were younger.

Gaund Ke Ladoo

Ingredients: (Makes 8-10)

- 1 cup gond (edible gum)
- 1 cup sooji
- 1 cup sugar
- 3 tbs ghee for frying

- **Optional:** green cardamom, raisins, cantaloupe seeds, coconut, poppy seeds, pistachios.

Method:

1. Fry the gond in a little hot ghee until it puffs up. Grind in food processor. Pass hard particles though sieve
2. Fry the sooji in a little ghee and toast it to darken a few shades.
3. Add the ground gond and sugar in the sooji and heat until sugar is melted.
4. Remove from heat and let it cool enough to handle.
5. Mix in the optional items. Make round balls and serve.

'Gond, gund, gaund' all mean edible gum resin that provides heat to the body. In winter or for nursing mothers during lactation, it has a very big following. Gaund ladoo comes in many variations including being made with whole wheat flour or with black pepper or ajwain or sonth (dry ginger). Gaund is also called paujeen in some parts of India. Seniors recommend this to new mothers because they have heard about the long term benefits of Gaund ke Ladoo. Being sweet and full of dry fruits has also encouraged its popularity.

Nan Khatai

Ingredients: (Makes 24)

- 1 cup maida (white flour)
- 1 cup very fine sooji (semolina)
- 1 cup besan (gram seed flour)
- 1 cup melted butter

- 1 cup sugar
- A pinch of ground cardamom
- A pinch of saffron

Method:

1. Mix all ingredients in a bowl to dough-like consistency.
2. Make small balls out of this dough and gently flatten them.
3. Put them in a non-stick tray.
4. Bake the balls at 350F for 15 to 20 minutes until they are golden in colour.
5. Take out balls and let them cool.
6. Nan khatai is ready to eat or store.

Dr. Virendra Jha came to Canada from India in 1969 to study and currently works at the Canadian Space Agency. His other interests include writing poetry. He has mastered this recipe which makes his Nan Khatais taste like the kind that one would find in India.

Safaid Ladoos

Ingredients: (Makes 12-16)

- 1 ½ cup semolina
- 2 cups khoya
- ¼ cup almonds
- ¼ cup pistachios
- 2 tbsp. cardamom – powder

- 1 ½ cups sugar
- ¾ cup ghee or unsalted butter
- Few drops of lemon juice

Method:

1. Soften the khoya by passing it through a sieve with large holes.
2. Roast semolina in ghee on low heat till it turns pinkish
3. Add khoya and roast for another 2-3 minutes. Remove from heat and cool.
4. Dissolve sugar in some water.
5. Return the vessel to heat and cook till the sugar syrup forms a two tread consistency (To test for doneness – take a bit of syrup in a spoon and press between forefinger and thumb to see if you get 2 strands of sugar).
6. Add drops of lemon juice. Cool and mix with the semolina and khoya.
7. Add the cardamom and nuts. Mix well and roll ladoos in small balls.

A yummy white ladoo is a celebrated favourite. In India, states are almost like countries themselves, each with their own language and dialect, own cuisine, traditions and customs. However, ladoos seem to roll all over the country in some form but the same shape and reasons for preparation are common. Festivities, wedding, offerings, prayers fasts, auspicious occasions, joyful events see some form of ladoo presentation. Many households in Kerela add coconut to this small snowball looking delights.

SNACKS AND STARTERS

One common factor in collecting these recipes was that the person giving them would estimate the measurements. Recipes had to be tested to determine the right proportion. Interestingly, how our seniors would say, "beta, pata nahin kitne dal na hai, tum andaze say dal do " (child, I don't know, just put by estimation). Many felt it was not in the ingredients, but rather a variation of the following that made a difference to the end result: the level of heat, length of time, thickness of pot, amount stirred, when to add spices, how to add them, temperature of the water to be added, when to add the salt, cooking a dish uncovered or covered, when to add garlic, how to chop the onion and many others.

One can tell how age and tajurba (experience) gave more to the dish than just following the steps of the recipe. Very highly emphasized by our elders is to enjoy cooking with a combination of "heart and feel", as well as eating fresh foods to get the maximum health benefits. Many also smile saying that in true Indian cuisine there really is nothing as 'appetizers', it's all part of one big meal!

Samosas

Ingredients: (Makes 12)

- **For filling:**
- 5 cups of ¼ inch cubed potatoes
- 1 2/3 cup peas - boiled
- 3 tbsp. ghee
- 2 tbsp. cumin seeds
- 3 tbsp. ginger -chopped
- 1 tsp. red chili- powder
- 1/3 cup coriander - chopped
- Lemon juice
- Salt to desired taste

- **For dough:**
- ¾ lbs. flour
- 4 tsp. peanut oil or canola oil
- (as some are peanut sensitive)
- Flour to dust
- Salt to desired taste

Method:

1. Sift flour and salt together. Add oil. When fully mixed add approximately 6 tbsp. water and knead gently to make a semi-hard dough. Cover with a moist cloth and let sit for 30 minutes. Divide into 6 portions.
2. Filling – Heat ghee. Add cumin seeds and brown them, then add ginger, potatoes, red chilies, and salt in sequence. Stir for 5 minutes. Reduce the heat to low, cover the pot, and cook until tender. Add lemon juice and boiled peas and stir until completely dry. Then let cool.
3. Roll dough approximately 8 inches in diameter and cut into half. Place the straight edge of the half moon along forefinger. Wet the edges with water-mixed-with-flour (i.e. to make a paste) and fold into a cone shape, pressing to form a seam. Stuff with potato filling and seal open edge. Fry samosas until they turn golden brown. Serve with Chutney or with ketchup.

As street food or at home, Indians just love samosas. Many different fillings such as chicken, keema, mixed vegetables, spinach, paneer, and dals are adaptations of this recipe. Some even mix ajwain, cumin or other spices to the dough. Nearly every house in Canada and India make these triangle snacks at home. Many now use readymade spring-roll wraps to substitute the home-made dough.

Pakoras

Ingredients: (Serves 4)

- **For Batter**
- 1 2/3 cup gram flour (besan)
- 1/3 tsp. baking soda
- ½ tsp. Cumin seeds
- 1 tsp. red chili – powder
- 2 tbsp. vegetable oil
- ¼ cup green coriander leaves - chopped
- 4 tbsp. lemon juice
- Oil to deep fry
- Salt to desired taste

- **Optional additions to batter:**
- Ajwain
- Amchur
- Green chillies-chopped
- Methi
- Onions
- **For Filling:**
- ½ kg of assorted vegetables (i.e. cauliflower, potatoes, onions, eggplant, spinach, green chili, fish, cooked chicken, paneer, etc.)

Method:

1. In a bowl, mix together all batter ingredients. Add approximately 200 ml of water until a consistency similar to a pancake mixture is obtained. Leave aside for 10 minutes.
2. Heat oil to smoking point and reduce to medium heat.
3. Deep-fry vegetables dipped in batter till golden brown or alternatively chop vegetables into small pieces and mix into the batter. Then drop spoonfuls into the hot oil.
4. Serve hot with ketchup, tamarind or coriander chutney.

This is a very common preparation all over India, especially on rainy days. This treat has many variations and sizes, especially when it comes to Paneer pakoras. Many people chop up assorted vegetables into small pieces and mix them into the batter to fry. All Pakoras can be half-fried and kept aside to deep fry again when all are ready to eat. Left-overs can be used in a vegetarian sandwich. Pakoras are a real hit and very well known to many Canadians, who look forward for them when visiting South Asian households. Many call them "Bhaji" as well.

Masala Peanuts

Ingredients: (Serves 2)

- ½ cup peanuts - salted
- 1 tsp. chili - powder
- ½ cup besan (Bengal gram flour)
- 2 tsp. fennel - powder (saunf)
- 1½ tsp. black salt

- 2-3 tbsp. water
- 1 tbsp. oil

Method:

1. Mix all these ingredients together in a bowl, ensuring the batter coats the peanuts evenly.
2. On a greased plate, spread the coated peanuts separately and microwave for 1 ½ minutes.

Mr. Dev Kaushal has perfected the art of Indian cooking in a microwave oven with amazing results. A wonderfully happy man in the kitchen, he tried to find ways to save time yet not compromise on taste. Even in his nineties he continued to make food and looked forward to his grandchildren's' visits to enjoy these with them.

Pakoras with Chutney

Tuna Cutlets

Ingredients: (Makes 2, or 4 small)

- 1 can of tuna - drained
- 1 onion – medium size, chopped fine
- 2 tbsp. bread crumbs – fully heaped
- 2 tbsp. green coriander leaves – finely chopped
- Salt to desired taste
- Oil for cooking

Method:

1. Mix all ingredients by hand in bowl.
2. Shape into round balls and flatten to make cutlets.
3. On medium-heat in a frying pan, add oil and fry both sides of cutlets till crisp and golden brown.
4. Put on a paper towel to absorb excess oil before serving.

Abne Ali Abidi has mastered this instant-hit cutlets recipe over the past 35 years. He says, "A good chutney on the side will have you licking your fingertips". He is very particular in all his food preparations and is a great host. He insists that one should "masal" (which means finely grinding by ones finger tips) the ingredients well, as the difference will show up in the taste. Many of our seniors express that it is not the ingredients, but the method, time and care given to food that gives it the good results.

Zucchini Squares

Ingredients: (Makes one 9"x12" pan)

- 3 cups of grated zucchini
- 1 cup chopped onion
- 2 tsp. chopped ginger
- 1 to 2 chopped green chilies
- ¾ cup Parmesan cheese
- 1 cup Bisquick

- 1/3 cup vegetable oil
- 4 eggs
- (No salt or pepper needed for this recipe)

Method:

1. In a bowl mix zucchini, onion, ginger, green chilies and parmesan cheese.
2. In another bowl, break eggs and stir with oil.
3. Pour bowl with eggs into the first bowl with all other ingredients. Add bisquick and mix well.
4. Spread the mixture out on a parchment paper-lined 9" x 12" pan.
5. Bake at 400 °F for 40 to 45 minutes.
6. Cut the mixture into squares and enjoy as is or with a cup of chai or salad. It makes for a healthy and nutritious meal.

Mrs. Sudarshan Bhatla came to Canada in 1962. Her skills to whip up healthy food items are to be marveled at. A retired teacher by profession, she recalls well how our Indian taste buds were largely compromised by lack of availability of specialized food items. Her carefully, calculated improvisation of recipes is a unique talent. She is a great inspiration to many by her commitment to maintaining a good, active health-style.

Aloo Tikki

Ingredients: (Serves 12)

- 1 kg potatoes - boiled
- 4.5 tbsp. corn flour
- Ghee to shallow-fry
- Salt to desired taste (approximately ½ tsp.)

- **For Filling:**
- 1 cup green peas
- 2 tbsp. ghee
- 1 tsp. cumin seeds
- 4 tsp. coriander - powder
- 1 tsp. red chili - powder

Method:

1. Peel and grate boiled potatoes. Add cornflower and salt. Mix well. Divide into 12 equal balls.
2. Heat ghee and cumin together. Heat till cumin crackles. Add peas, stir and add the remaining ingredients. Cool and mash peas. Fill pea mixture into potatoes to make patties. Shallow fry until patties turn golden brown.

Another very popular street food, many variations have cropped up with an amazing variety of fillings: ground cooked meat, roasted vegetables, paneer, tofu, corn, etc. Seniors shared that in India, they would love to go for a walk with their families and have some chaat and aloo tikkies served on bowls made from peepal or banyan leaves. To remember the tikkiwala (street vendor,) split open the hot tikkis in two and pour yummy chutneys on top of them and serve them with a small, wooden spoon that makes many mouths water.

Ragda Patties

Ingredients: (Makes 8)

- 2 cups white peas – soaked
- 4 potatoes – boiled
- 1/2 cups rava
- 1 cup breadcrumbs
- 10 green chilies
- 1 tbsp. coriander
- 1 tbsp. mint

- ½ tsp. cumin powder
- ½ tsp. pepper powder
- ½ tsp. turmeric powder
- ½ tsp. garam masala
- Oil for frying
- Salt to desired taste

Method:

1. Cook ¼ cup of white peas in a pressure cooker with some salt.
2. Add coriander, mint and chopped green chilies.
3. Blend it well to make a paste.
4. Mix cumin powder, turmeric powder and garam masala.
5. Fry it for few more minutes. Add peas and water.
6. Boil until it turns thick. Ragda is ready.
7. Mash the boiled potatoes.
8. Mix mashed potatoes, breadcrumbs, rava, green chilies, turmeric powder and salt to make it into a light dough.
9. Make flat round patties from the dough.
10. Bake them at 350°F until they turn crisp or brown with a little oil in a hot pan till golden in color.
11. Pour ragda on hot patties.
12. Serve with green, red and imli chutneys on top of the ragda.

Malika Gandhi migrated to Canda in 1976 from Gwalior, Madhya Pradesh, and is very active in the Gujarati and the Indian communities. This active grandmother teaches aqua fitness and loves to organize Gujarati community events. She can make many people happy by cooking in large quantites the patties or her famous gol guppas.

Raj Kachori

Ingredients: (Serves 8)

- 2 cups rava
- 2 tbsp. white flour
- 4 potatoes
- 1 cup curd
- ½ cup channa - soaked
- 10 papdi

- 1 tsp. roasted cumin – powder
- 1 tsp. red chili –powder
- 5 tbsp. tamarind chutney
- ½ cup sev

Method:

1. Boil the potatoes and cut them into cubes.
2. Boil the soaked channa.
3. Mix rava, maida, salt and red chili powder.
4. Prepare dough with prepared ingredients.
5. Roll out into rotis of equal size and deep fry them.
6. Make a hole in the centre of the fried kachoris.
7. Fill with cubed potatoes, chana, papdi and curd.
8. Spread red chili powder, cumin seed powder, tamarind chutney and green chutney.
9. Put sev on it. Ready to serve.

This is a festive chaat item and a real eye pleaser. However, this is not often made at home unlike its substitute "Chaat Papri" as it is more time consuming and often eaten out at 'chaat stalls'.

Matri (Mathri)

Ingredients: (Makes 24)

- 1 kg flour – all purpose
- 250 gm butter
- 1 ½ tbsp. Ajwain
- ¼ cup oil

- 1 ½ tbsp. black pepper - coarse
- Warm water
- Salt to desired taste

Method:

1. Mix all the dry ingredients.
2. Add enough warm water to make a semi-stiff yet smooth dough.
3. Make 1" balls from dough and roll into ¼" inch discs with rolling pin.
4. With a fork, prick a few holes on both sides to avoid the dough from puffing. Allow to dry a few minutes.
5. Deep-fry in hot oil at medium heat until matti is golden brown in colour.
6. Cool and store in a sealed container for up to 3 weeks. Enjoy with tea or pickles.

Jagdish Kaur has been making these for years. Learnt these in Nairobi, and enjoys making them in England as well as in Canada. This Rajasthani tea snack is enjoyed during festivities, weddings or fasts. A laborious job to make, ladies would turn this into a socializing event where they would make large batches together to take back to their homes, also allowing time to be spent with their friends. Here, she enjoys making them with her sister in law for samagams at the Gurudwara .

Zucchini Soup

Ingredients: (Serves 6)

- 2 lbs. zucchini
- 31/2 cups vegetable broth
- 2 tsp. oil
- 1 medium sized onion - chopped
- 1 tsp. ginger - grated
- 1 tsp. coriander leaves - chopped
- 2 tsp. curry - powder
- ½ tsp. black pepper
- 1 cup yoghurt (room temp)

Method:

1. Heat oil in a pan on medium heat and fry the onions.
2. Add ginger and green coriander, curry powder, salt and pepper, stir.
3. Add sliced zucchini. Cook and stir for 5 minutes till zucchini looses firmness and becomes soft.
4. Add the broth and bring to boil. Reduce heat and simmer till veggies are soft (approx. 10 min).
5. Remove pot from heat and cool.
6. With hand-blender puree the mix.
7. Add a bit of mix to the yoghurt in order to equalize the temperature, then add the yoghurt to pureed soup. Stir continuously with hand blender to prevent yoghurt from separating.
8. Heat and serve.

Abne Ali Abidi really enjoys making this soup and sharing it's details. He prefers yogurt to give it a tangy flavor but his wife prefers it without that. His enthusiasm is very contagious and he is a remarkable story teller - the joy in his giving details becomes a story by itself. Since he introduced the zucchini soup, Aangan's seniors have already began to make this recipe in the winter and are appreciative to have gotten it from us after loving its samplings.

Tofu Kabab

Ingredients: (Makes 6-8)

- 1 lb firm, grated tofu
- 3 tbsp. roasted besan
- 4 tbsp. breadcrumbs
- 2 large boiled potatoes
- 4 green chilies – chopped
- 2 tsp. ginger – grated
- 1 chopped medium-sized onion
- 1 cup of fresh green coriander
- 1 tsp. chili powder
- 1 tsp. coarsely ground cumin seeds
- 2 finely-chopped celery sticks
- Salt and pepper to desired taste

Method:

1. Mix all ingredients well.
2. Make round patties of the mix.
3. Pan fry both sides of the patties until golden brown with the help of a little bit of oil.
4. Serve with green chili chutney.

Amita Khanna has been a very active member of the community for over 30 years; taking care of children, working in the YMCA and teaching Hindi. Making unusually tasty food seems to come to her naturally. Chetan Talwar, one of her many students, has helped put this recipe together along with her chicken parantha recipe. She is a very happy grandmother who is always willing to give a helping hand.

Fenugreek (Methi) Salad

Ingredients: (Serves 2)

- 150 gm Fenugreek leaves
- 1 medium-sized tomato
- 1 medium-sized onion
- 1 tbsp. of cumin seeds
- 1 tbsp. of lemon juice
- ½ tbsp. garam masala
- ½ tbsp. of red chilli
- ½ tbsp. of black pepper
- 2 green chilies
- Salt to desired taste

Method:

1. Wash Fenugreek leaves well and dry, before chopping to bite sized pieces.
2. Chop the tomato, onion and green chilli finely, mix all ingredients with garam masala, red chilies, salt and pepper and serve.

Fenugreek, with its very nutritious value, has found a home in the hearts of many seniors who cannot stop singing its praises. A rare salad item with numerous health benefits not made often enough.

Tuk

Ingredients: (Makes 12)

- 3 large white potatoes
- Oil for frying
- 1 teaspoon Amchur powder
- ½ teaspoon red chilli powder
- ½ teaspoon dhaniya powder
- Salt to desired taste

Method:

1. Peel and cut potatoes into large chunks, wash and drain off water.
2. Salt the damp potatoes.
3. Heat oil in large pot, shake off excess liquid off the potatoes and put into hot oil.
4. Cook potatoes on medium heat so they cook through but not brown. They should be a very light golden brown. Remove them onto a paper towel or colander to drain excess oil. Repeat this until the potatoes are cooked and cool to lukewarm.
5. Squash to press the potatoes between your palms or on board, to about ½ inch in thickness.
6. Increase temperature of the oil to refry the potatoes a second time. This will create a very crispy golden brown crust on potatoes.
7. Remove potatoes onto paper towel and sprinkle with the 3-spice blend and serve hot.
8. Enjoy!

Originally from London, England and having migrated to Canada, Mrs. Vijay Jadwani has mastered the art of Sindhi cooking. This very tasty dish compares to French fries and is very popular with the youth. Pronounced "Touq"

Sprout Chaat

Ingredients: (Serves 4)

- 1 lb. green whole moong dal
- 1 tsp. haldi (turmeric)
- 1 tsp. cucumber – finely chopped
- 1 tsp. green mango - finely chopped
- 1 tsp. spring onion - finely chopped
- 1 tsp. tomatoes - finely chopped
- 1 tsp. potatoes - boiled, finely chopped
- 1 tsp. green chilies - finely chopped
- 1 tsp. green coriander - finely chopped
- 2 tbsp. lemon juice or tamarind water
- Salt and red chilies to desired taste

Method:

1. Wash and soak the dal. Drain and cover with wet cloth for 2 days in winter. Make sure the cloth stays wet. By keeping the dal in an oven where the temperature is warmer, sprouting time is reduced. (In the summer, a sunny spot is favorable as it reduces sprouting time by an entire day). Raise the sprouts.
2. In a large pot put water to boil, add the haldi and salt.
3. Once the water comes to a good boil, add the sprouts and remove from water as soon as the water boils again. This does not cook the sprouts but it removes the rawness of the sprouts in the boiling water. (You can drink this nutritious water or use it for other preparation where water is required, especially when cooking dal, making atta or curry).
4. Cook the sprouts and handle with care, to not break them.
5. Add and mix all the ingredients except the green coriander.
6. Serve and garnish with fresh green coriander.

Manpreet Malik is known for making amazing sprouts in our community. Her expert method is different than spreading the dal out flat to sprout. Her recipe has many variations, for example, adding chopped apples or nuts. Her recipe is enjoyed by her grandchild as well as many seniors. Since the seventies she has loved to cook and now finds many food products more readily available which helps in making the real stuff. Her helping hands serve community where she happily brings homemade pickles and treats.

Yummilicious Masala Corn

Ingredients: (Serves 2)

- 1 cup corn kernels (canned or fresh)
- 1 tsp. salted butter
- 1 tsp. lime juice
- 1 tsp. chunky chat masala

Method:

1. Mix the corn and butter in a bowl and microwave on high for 2 minutes.
2. Add lime juice and chunky chat masala, and mix well. Enjoy it warm.
3. Serve it as a delicious snack!

Mrs. Poonia, in her late sixties, makes this corn snack which is a great hit with her grand children. During the process of making this cookbook, her 12 year old granddaughter insisted that this masala corn recipe must be included. She has enjoyed this so much on her visits to India and she wants her grandmother to make it as often as possible when here.

MAIN DISHES

Many of our seniors saw the invention of radios, cameras, computers, television and household appliances. Many of them flew for the first time in an airplane while migrating to Canada in hopes of a better life, for work, or to be with family that was already here. It is endearing to see how many of them fondly remember the first "meri mixey" (my blender) in their kitchens in the 60s, this seemed like a God given gift as it really aided in cutting down preparation time. All these gadgets (although the microwave is still not really appreciated by some), are very helpful tools in reducing time, so that the family has more time to sit and enjoy eating a meal. Eating together is very important and sadly not done often enough our seniors say. Now they are also happy to find many familiar fruits and vegetables readily available. This is very different than having to go to the only south-Asian grocery store in Montreal in the 1970's that sometimes sold green coriander.

A note: in our recipes we do not have any dal preparations. This is perhaps odd, as it is the most common main dish, accompanying most meals. Many of the seniors are vegetarians and dal is an important source of protein, also a very basic comfort food. Made in an infinite number of ways, a cookbook of dal recipes combined could be thicker than an encyclopedia. Not being able to do justice to the dal preparations, we suggest that you sit with the elders in your families and enrich your lives and diets by their fond memories and their many daal recipes!

A note on Curry: A general misconception is that 'curry' is one type of dish, whereas curry can translate into a thousand different dishes, each with their own taste and consistency.

The word "curry" comes from the Tamil "kari" or the Marathi 'kadi" (a type of thick sauce). Curry translates to one, and one thing alone– a dish that has 'gravy'!

It can be a semi-dry, thick or runny. It can have a smooth or chunky texture. These curries are usually based on some combination of water, yoghurt, coconut milk, tomato puree, stock or cream. "Curry" is the sauce one scoops up in their roti or mixes in the rice to moisten the food which allows the flavors blend in the bite to be consumed.

Many have heard or seen boxes labeled "curry powder" which is a generic replacement for the more flavorful original dry mixture of red chilies, coriander, cumin, turmeric and fenugreek. This commercially prepared mixture of spices is thought to have been prepared by Indian merchants in the 18th century to sell to the British headed back to England. Many of us individuals who migrated to Canada came to know of its existence only after arrival. The truth is, curry powder does not exist in daily household cooking in South Asian kitchens – the spices are added to the curry depending on the requirement of the recipe. In making this cookbook our seniors wanted to convey that enjoying whole natural spices as they are, will certainly result in the better tasting dish. No 'curry powder' can beat the real stuff!

Muttar Paneer

Ingredients: (Serves 6)

- 200 gms paneer– cubed (substitute: Ricotta)
- 250 gms green peas
- 2 large onions - ground to paste
- 1 tbsp.ginger - paste
- 2 tbsp. garlic - paste
- 2 tsp. coriander - powder
- 1 tsp. cumin - powder
- ½ tsp. turmeric - powder
- 2 green chillies - chopped

- 4 tbsp. oil
- 1 tsp. whole cumin seeds
- 1 ½ cup warm water
- 2 tbsp. tomato paste
- 3 tomatoes - medium-sized
- 3 tbsp. green coriander leaves - chopped
- 1 tsp. garam masala
- Salt to desired taste

Method:

1. On a hot non-stick pan with no oil, grill paneer/ricotta pieces until they become brown. Keep aside (traditional way is to fry the paneer cubes).
2. Heat oil in a pot and add cumin seeds until they become brown. Add onion paste to the oil and stir until brown. Then add garlic and ginger paste. Grind tomatoes in a blender, add to mixture and heat for 2 minutes until they turn reddish brown.
3. Add coriander, cumin, turmeric, garam masala and green chilies to mixture and stir continuously until oil begins to separate from mixture.
4. Add green peas and stir for 2 to 3 minutes.
5. Add water and salt and bring the mixture to simmer.
6. Add grilled paneer/ricotta pieces and when the gravy is as thick or thin as you like, turn off the heat.
7. Garnish the dish with chopped green coriander leaves.

Paramjit Singh has mastered this recipe over the past 35 years. Her version of replacing paneer with ricotta gives better results than using store bought paneer. Since she had to cut off fat due to health reasons, she found a way to grill ricotta/paneer instead of frying it. Even for her Kadhi, she broils falafel balls to avoid frying process and succeeded in making a good alternative to pakoras, while not compromising the taste.

Malai Kofta

Ingredients: (Serves 4)

- **For Koftas:**
  - 1 cup paneer - crumbled
  - 1 tbsp. flour (maida)
  - A pinch of baking powder
  - 2 green chillies-finely, chopped
  - 2 tbsp. green coriander leaves -chopped
  - Salt to desired taste
- **For Paste:**
  - ½ cup onions - sliced
  - 3 garlic cloves - peeled
  - 2 green chilies

- **For Gravy:**
  - 4 red tomatoes - medium-sized
  - 1 cup whole milk
  - ¼ cup 35% cream
  - 1 tbsp. Kasoori methi
  - 1 tbsp. oil
  - Salt to desired taste
  - 3 dried red chilies
  - 2 tsp. coriander seeds
  - 1 tsp. cumin seeds
  - 1 inch fresh ginger piece
  - 2 cloves
  - 1 inch cinnamon stick

Method:

Koftas:
1. Mix paneer, maida, baking powder, green chilies, coriander and salt. Shape mixture into small balls.
2. On a greased plate, microwave balls for 45 seconds

Gravy:
1. Pierce tomatoes with fork and microwave for 4 minutes. Cool and puree tomatoes.
2. In another bowl, add oil and ground paste. Microwave for 5 minutes.
3. Add tomato puree to 2), stir and microwave for 3 minutes.
4. Stir once and add mild, cream, Kasoori methi and salt and microwave 2 minutes longer.
5. Just before serving, add koftas to gravy and microwave for 2 minutes.
6. Garnish with green coriander leaves and serve.

Mr. Devinder Dev Kaushal's passion for cooking for himself and others was rewarding. Taking notes of his recipes is worthy of praise and his koftas are as well remembered as he is. To see him enjoy himself while preparing his dishes was pure joy as he adapted most of his recipes to the changing technology which fascinated all of us. We salute him.

Punjabi Kadhi

Ingredients: (Serves 6-8)

- **For Kadhi:** ←——————————→ **For Pakoras:**
- 250 grams spinach
- 250 grams besan
- 3 tbsp. green coriander - chopped
- 1 large potato - chopped
- 1 tbsp. ginger -chopped
- 2 green chilies - chopped
- 1 tsp. lemon juice
- Oil to deep fry
- Salt to desired taste

- 1 kg yogurt
- 1 tbsp. turmeric
- ½ cup besan
- 1 tsp. red chili powder
- 2 tsp. coriander powder
- 1 tsp. cumin powder
- 1 tbsp. methi -dry
- A pinch of asafoetida (hing)
- 2 tablespoons garlic - chopped
- 1 tablespoon ginger - chopped
- 2 medium-sized onions - chopped
- 2-3 green chilies
- 4 tablespoons oil
- Salt to desired taste

Method:

1. Put oil in a pot at medium-heat. Add onions and stir. Stir in garlic and ginger, cook until brown.
2. Slowly add a combined mixture of yoghurt, besan and turmeric into the oil. Make sure to keep it stirred until it boils otherwise the curd will separate from the whey. A very important step is to stir till kadhi boils.
3. Add red chilies, ground coriander, cumin powder, methi and heeng.
4. Simmer on low heat until the mixture is thick and lustrous. Add warm water to thin mixture, if needed.
5. Make pakoras by mixing besan with water to make thick paste. Add all other ingredients and mix. Keep aside 10 minutes. Add salt right before frying. Deep fry spoonfuls of pakoras in hot oil.
6. Drain the oil and add pakoras to kadhi.

Sarla Devi Puri was born in Ludharia, Punjab in 1916. She learnt to make this dish from her mom. Once married, her in-laws relished it. This 96 year old senior has taught this recipe to her 70-year old daughter, Rajni Khanna, who is well known in our community for making one of the best curries and for being a helpful community volunteer.

Goat Curry

Ingredients: (Serves 6-8)

- 1 kg. goat meat with bones, cubed
- 4 tbsp. oil
- 2 black cardamom
- One cinnamon stick - 2 inch
- 6 cloves
- 3 large onions ground up
- 3 tbsp. garlic paste
- 3 tbsp. ginger paste

- 5 large tomatoes
- 2 tsp. turmeric
- 1 tsp. red chilies
- Salt to desired taste
- 1 ½ tsp. garam masala
- 2 chopped green chilies
- ¼ cup chopped green coriander leaves
- Hot water

Method:

1. In a heavy bottom pan heat oil. Add black cardamom, cinnamon stick and cloves and cook until flavours are released.
2. Add ground onions and stir on medium-low heat.
3. Add garlic and ginger paste. Brown the mixture until the oil separates.
4. Put tomatoes in hot water until skin is easy to peel skins, then chop . Add these to the mixture and cook until brown.
5. Add turmeric, red chillies, salt and stir.
6. Add washed, dried meat and brown it slowly.   Keep browning and stir often. Bhunno (or brown) the meat until the smell of the meat is gone and you can smell the flavour of the masala.
7. Once roasted, add hot water to produce the desired amount of gravy and add a little more since the water will evaporate while cooking.
8. Simmer the mixture until the meat is soft but do not overcook.
9. Add green chilies, garam masala and green coriander leaves.

At 76, Mrs. Jogender Kaur Bhatia still loves seeing the joy of her family when they eat this age-old tried and tested recipe. She assures that by replacing the goat meat with boned chicken, one can produce an equally amazing chicken curry.

Saag

Ingredients: (Serves 6)

- 2 bunches rapini - chopped
- 3 bunches spinach -chopped
- ½ broccoli – chopped (optional)
- 1 small white turnip – chopped (optional)
- 2 tbsp. methi
- 1 large, whole garlic – grated
- 1 tbsp. besan or Maki ka Atta

- Tadka (tempering)
- 4 green chilies - chopped
- 1 tsp. red chili - powder
- 1 onion - medium- sized, chopped
- 2 inch piece of ginger - chopped
- 4 tbsp. oil or ghee
- White butter (optional)

Method:

1. Cook rapini, spinach, broccoli, methi and turnip with garlic and salt in covered pot on low heat.
2. Simmer in juices until vegetables are soft. Add besan flour or Maki ka Atta. Mash the mixture to puree texture. Cook until desired thickness is attained.
3. In another pot, heat oil/ghee. Once hot, add the onions and cook till brown. Add red chili powder, ginger and green chilies. Remove from heat. Add onions to saag.
4. Top the dish with butter when serving if you desire.

To make white butter:

Ingredient: 35% cream

Put cream in food processor and blend 2-3 minutes. It will turn smooth and then the buttermilk will separate from butter. Put few ice cubes to harden butter and pass it through the sieve. Keep a bowl to gather the buttermilk to use for curry, pancake batter or muffin mix.

Lila Vati Sharma was reputed for her delicious cooking and her generosity. Authentic saag is best accompanied with white butter on top. To date, in most traditional home and villages, it is served with it. She traveled to Canada from Nairobi and is remembered for her love of gardening. She grew and cooked her own home grown greens and is dearly missed.

Lamb Curry: Guyanese Style

Ingredients: (Serves 6)

- 2 lbs lamb cubes (boneless)
- 1 small onion (minced)
- 3-4 cloves of garlic (minced)
- 1 tbsp. Curry powder
- 1tbsp. Garam masala
- 1 small potato peeled and cut into cubes
- 1 tbsp vegetable oil
- 1-2 cloves
- 1 small piece of cinnamon
- Water for gravy

Method:

1. Wash cubes of meat thoroughly. Drain.
2. Make a paste with onions, garlic, garam masala and curry powder. Add some water for paste.
3. Heat oil, add the cloves and spices. As they splutter add the masala paste.
4. Sauté for 3 minutes, then add the lamb. Sauté in a wide covered pot until all the water is evaporated on medium heat.
5. Add potatoes after water has evaporated to meat and sauté for 5 more minutes.
6. Add more water to completely cook the meat and potatoes.
7. Enjoy with rice or naan

Shira Haniff's great great grandfather migrated from India to Guyana from the Punjab region and is of Muslim descent. At 80 years of age it is remarkable to see her spirit and energy. In the summer of 2011, in the backyard of her daughter's home in Baie-D'urfe, she was happily cooking away this recipe for about a 100 people.

Mogo Cassava

Ingredients: (Serves 6)

- 2 packets of frozen cassava (500 grams each packet)
- 2 tsp lemon juice
- 2 tsp salt
- 2 tsp coriander powder
- ¾ tsp turmeric
- 1.5 liter water
- 2 tbsp oil
- Finely chopped fresh coriander (handful)
- Finely chopped green chilies (optional)

Method:

1. Heat water in a 4L pressure cooker.
2. Rinse cassava in warm water to remove the ice and put in pressure cooker
3. Cook on high heat for two full whistles.
4. Turn off stove and let the pressure cooker cool off, until the pressure releases.
5. Take out the cassava pieces and remove the roots by hand.
6. Cut or mash the cassava into small bite-size pieces and put back into the pot.
7. Add the salt, coriander powder, turmeric, oil and lemon juice.
8. Mix well with a large spoon (add more boiling water to the mixture if the consistency is too dry).
9. Pour into bowls and top with fresh coriander (and green chilies).

Mrs. Shardha Patni was born in Madagascar, lived in Kenya and migrated to Canada in the early 1970's. Her grandparents were from India. This recipe holds its roots in Madagascar and is thoroughly enjoyed by Mrs. Patni's grandchildren.

Cauliflower Rasam

Ingredients: (Serves 4-6)

- 4 or 5 florets of 2cm width cauliflower -
- 2 to 3 Tbsp Toor dal –cooked
- 1 Tomato (large) chopped small
- 1 Onion (medium) chopped fine
- 2 Green chilies
- 1/4 tsp Saunf
- 2 pieces ½"Cinnamon stick
- 4 - 5 Pepper pods
- 1/2 tsp. Mustard seeds
- 1 Bay leaf
- 6 -7 Curry leaves
- 2 tbsp. Chopped coriander leaves
- 1/2 tsp. Turmeric powder
- water

Method:

1. Add about 2 tsp. cooking oil in a pan. When hot add green chilies, saunf, cinnamon, pepper pods, mustard seeds and bay leaf.
2. When the mustard splutters add onion and cook on medium heat until onion becomes transparent.
3. Add chopped tomatoes and turmeric and cook until tender.
4. Add the cooked dal and cauliflower and cook until cauliflower is just done. Add about 1 to 11/2 cups of water and salt to taste. Boil well.
5. Remove from heat and add about 1/4 cup of 2% milk. Add coriander leaves.
6. Serve like soup or serve it with hot rice.

Bhanu Jayakumar shares this soup which is not that well known, but thoroughly enjoyed by her friends in Montreal. It is soothing to end a meal with. This Chettinad recipe was shared with her by a Montreal based South-Indian friend of hers.

South Indian Chicken Korma

Ingredients: (Serves 4-6)

- 1 Whole chicken, cut into 2" pieces, without skin and washed well.
- 3 Tomatoes large –in 2cm cubes
- 1 1/2 Onion medium - sliced thin
- 2 Green Chillies
- 1 tbsp. Coriander powder
- 3 tbsp. Coconut milk powder dissolved in about 1/2 cup warm water
- 2 tsp. Chili powder
- Salt to taste
- 1 tsp. mustard seeds
- 1/4 tsp. pepper pods
- 10 curry leaves
- 2tbs Poppy seeds
- 1tbs fennel seeds
- 1" cinnamon stick

- **Masala paste :**
- Grind following to a fine paste with water:
- 10 cloves garlic (chopped)
- 1" piece ginger (chopped
- 5 pods cardamom
- 6 Cloves

Method:

1. Marinate chicken with sufficient salt, 1 tsp. chili powder and 1/2 tsp turmeric and set aside in fridge for about an hour.
2. Heat cooking oil (about 2 tbsp.) in a heavy bottomed Dutch oven. Add a bay leaf, a piece of cinnamon stick, 2 cardamoms and 2 cloves..
3. Add onions and green chilies and cook on medium heat until onion becomes transparent.
4. Add masala paste and cook for a couple of minutes.
5. Add tomatoes and marinated chicken to this and cook on medium heat stirring the chicken around occasionally.
6. Close the pot and adjust heat and cook until the chicken is done.
7. Add coriander powder and chili powder and boil well?.
8. Finally add the dissolved coconut milk powder until the chicken just returns to a boil.
9. Turn off heat.
10. Heat a tsp. of oil in a pan. Add poppy seeds, fennel seeds and cinnamon stick
11. Add to the chicken and garnish with chopped coriander leaves.
12. Serve with hot rice, pulao, Nan or chapattis

Bhanu Jayakumar is delighted to share her mother's famous Nagercoil (in Tamil) Chicken korma recipe which has reached Montreal through her. She is always asked to bring this dish for potluck dinners with her friends. She mentioned that coconut milk powder is available in Indian stores in Montreal and much better to use than coconut milk which is too thick for this dish.

Muttar Keema

Ingredients: (Serves 6)

- 500 gms. washed keema (minced lamb or beef)
- 250 gm peas (frozen/fresh)
- 3-4 tbsp. oil
- 1 tsp. cumin seed
- 2 black cardamoms
- 2 cloves
- 1 inch cinnamon stick
- 2 diced medium-sized onions
- 5 thinly-sliced cloves of garlic
- 1 tsp. turmeric powder
- 3 tbsp. ground coriander
- Red chili powder to desired taste (usually ½ to 1 tsp)
- Pinch of cinnamon
- ½ inch diced ginger
- ½ tsp. ground cumin seed
- 1 tsp. garam masala
- 2 cups of water (approximately)
- Handful fresh green coriander leaves
- Salt and pepper to desired taste

Method:

1. Add oil to a medium-sized pot and bring to med-high heat. When oil is heated well, add cumin seed, cardamom, cinnamon stick, and cloves. Wait few seconds, and then add diced onions, garlic, and ginger. Sauté for 2 minutes. Stir continuously till this masala paste begins to turn brown.
2. Add turmeric powder, coriander powder, red chili powder, salt, and cumin seed powder to paste. Add 4 tbsp of water to the masala and stir continuously till mix becomes reddish brown and oil gets separated in pan.
3. Bring heat to low-medium, and add meat to pan. Stir continuously. Bring heat to medium-high and roast meat for 5 minutes.
4. Add whole green peas. Stir.
5. Add 1 to 1 1/2 cup water till keema is completely soaked in water.
6. Cover the pan and cook for 7 minutes at medium–high heat and the 5 minutes at low heat.
7. Add garam masala and stir while adding so that the masala doesn't stick to bottom of pan.
8. Garnish with coriander and serve

Mrs. Chitra Srivastava learned this recipe from her mother in India. While living in Montreal, she edited the recipe according to her children's and husbands taste. She says that the bit of cinnamon that she adds to the dish enhances its aroma and flavor (a Canadian trick that she picked up). This Keema is still enjoyed immensely by her children.

Dosa

Ingredients: (Serves 6)

- **For Dosa:**
  - 4 cups of rice
  - 1 cup of Urad dal
  - 1 tsp. of methi (fenugreek) seeds
  - Salt to desired taste
  - Oil for cooking

- **For Filling:**
  - 10 medium Boiled and roughly smashed potatoes
  - 1 tsp Haldi
  - 2 tsp Lemon juice
  - 1 tsp Mustard seeds
  - ½ tsp Red chillies
  - 1 tbp Channa daal, washed
  - 2 dozen Curry leaves
  - Salt to taste
  - 4 tsp oil

Method:

1. Soak rice overnight in water.
2. Separately, soak dal overnight in water with methi seeds.
3. Grind the rice and dal into a fine paste.
4. Mix both by using your hands with the addition of salt.
5. Let the rice-dal dough rise for 2 hours or longer with yeast.
6. Before making the dosas, mix the batter again.
7. Heat a clean flat tawa (flat grill). Pour dosa batter on it and spread in circular motion to create a dosa, like a crepe. (If tawa is too hot, batter will clump together and stick)
8. Drizzle oil on to the top to cook the bottom surface of the dosa until it is very crisp.
9. Roll and serve plain dosa or fill with potato mixture.
10. Potato filling is made by heating 4 tsp oil, adding rai seeds, channa dal, curry leaves and red chili. Once mustard seeds pop, add potato. Add haldi and stir. Add lemon juice and salt, top with green coriander and green chillies.

Prema Venugopalan came to Canada in 1966 and is a well known spiritual teacher in the community. Though born in Kerala, she grew up in Calcutta with exposure to Bengali culture. She finds that somehow mixing the batter by hand rather than a wooden spoon, the dosa batter turns out better. The first dosa seems is always a trail as it seals well the tawa for the other dosas to be made. Some people use an half cut onion to wipe the hot tawa to keep the dosa's from sticking to it's surface.

Butter Chicken

Ingredients: (Serves 6-8)

- **For Chicken:**
  - 4 cups boneless chicken pieces
  - 4 tbsp. yogurt
  - 2 tbsp. 15 or 35% cream
  - 1 tsp. kasoori methi
  - 2 tbsp. butter
  - 4 tsp. lemon juice
  - 1 tsp. cumin powder
  - 1 tsp. chilli powder
  - 2 tsp. ginger-garlic paste
  - ½ tsp. garam masala
  - 1 tsp. salt
  - A pinch of red food colouring

- **For Gravy:**
  - 1 cup chopped onions
  - 1 cup chopped tomatoes
  - 1 tsp. chillies
  - 1 tsp. ginger-garlic paste
  - 2 tbsp. ground cashew
  - ¼ tsp. garam masala
  - 4 tbsp. butter
  - 1 tsp. kasoori methi
  - ½ tsp. cumin powder
  - ½ tsp. sugar
  - ¼ cup 15% or 35% cream
  - A pinch of red food colouring
  - Salt to desired taste

Method:

1. Marinate the chicken pieces with the given "ingredients for chicken" and refrigerate overnight, or a minimum of 3 hours. (Note: Many use store bought tandoori masala and mix it with the yogurt marinade).
2. Bake the chicken on trays for 15 minutes at 425F.
3. Then, broil chicken 7 to 9 minutes until the oil starts to separate.
4. Do not discard the juices.
5. In a heavy pan, heat the butter and sauté the onions until they are translucent.
6. Add ginger-garlic paste and stir.
7. Add chillies, garam masala and tomatoes and stir until the tomatoes turn soft.
8. Cool mixture and add to blender with cashews, to make a fine smooth paste.
9. In a pan, bring the mixture to boil with ½ cup of water. Simmer for 10 minutes and stir occasionally.
10. Add sugar, cream, salt, food colouring and chicken pieces to the mixture.
11. Simmer until the butter chicken consistency is reached.
12. Turn off the heat and add the butter, Kasoori methi and cumin powder.
13. Top the dish with green coriander and chopped green chillies if you like.

Butter chicken is one of most loved and famous Indian cuisine dishes. It is said that butter chicken was first created in the 1950s at "Moti Mahal", a Delhi restaurant famous for making Tandoori chicken; the chef recycled the juices leftover in the trays from the tandoori chicken pieces, then mixed these juices along with tomatoes and butter to make a sauce – voila, butter chicken was invented! Though it does not have much butter in its contents, the satin smoothness of the dish is what gives it its name. A senior lovingly recalls that in the early sixties her nanaji (grandfather) would drive the entire family in his black, shiny Austin to Moti Mahal nearly every month for years in a row. There he would listen to the Quawaali singers, while his family enjoyed the foods. She had no idea till recently, that, what she was enjoying then, was the real, original butter chicken! Different seniors here are well known for making their own way this favorite dish with much pride. We experimented to get the one best possible result for our youth. Enjoy !

Rajma

Ingredients: (Serves 6)

- ½ tsp. cumin seed
- 3 cups red kidney beans
- 4 tomatoes medium sized - chopped
- 2 onions medium sized - finely chopped
- 2 tbsp. oil
- 2 tsp. tomato paste
- ¾ tsp. turmeric powder
- 2 tsp. coriander powder
- 1 tsp. garam masala
- ½ tsp. red chilli powder (to desired taste)

- 2 tsp. fresh coriander leaves
- 2-inch cinnamon stick
- 3 dried bay leaves
- 2 finely-chopped garlic cloves
- ½ tsp. of ginger powder
- 4 whole black peppers
- 2 whole green chilies
- Salt to desired taste
- (Optional: ½ tsp. MDH brand Rajma powder)

Method:

1. Wash beans and soak them for 6-8 hours in water in a pressure cooker. Make sure one inch of water covers the top of the beans.
2. Add bay leafs, black pepper, cinnamon stick and salt to the pressure cooker.
3. Cook the beans on high-heat for 2 whistles.
4. After 2 whistles, reduce to medium-low heat and cook beans for 10-12 minutes.
5. In a saucepan, heat oil at medium-heat and add onions, cumin seeds, ginger and garlic and cook till onions are reddish.
6. Add the tomato paste to the mixture and stir on medium-heat for 2 more minutes.
7. Add turmeric, coriander powder, red chilli powder and garam masala and cook and stir the mixture.
8. When the oil separates from the masala in the mixture, add boiled beans with water (note: canned red kidney beans may be added alternatively here) and 2 whole green chillies to the saucepan. If the consistency is too thick for your liking, add some water.
9. Stir the rajma nicely and simmer for 10 minutes.
10. Garnish with green coriander on to
11. Serve with rice or roti and enjoy!

Asha Khare has been making this recipe for her children for over 30 years. They enjoy it immensely. It is a tasty and healthy dish high in protein. Canned red kidney beans can also be used with this recipe if you don't have a pressure cooker or don't have time to pre-soak and boil the beans.

Aloo Rasa

Ingredients: (Serves 2)

- 1 large boiled potato
- ¼ tsp cumin seeds
- pinch of hing
- ¼ turmeric powder
- red chili to taste
- 1 large chopped tomato

- 1 Tbs grated ginger
- 1 ½ cup water
- 1 chopped green chili
- 2 tsp chopped green coriander
- salt to taste
- 2 tbsp oil or ghee

Method:

1. Heat oil or ghee in pot over medium heat.
2. Add cumin seeds and pinch of hing until seeds are roasted
3. Add potato, turmeric, red chili, chopped tomatoes, ginger and stir
4. Add water and simmer on low heat for about 15 minutes
5. Add salt to taste
6. Remove off heat and add green chilies and coriander before serving

Yash Verma can make this recipe blindfolded. A family favorite, especially served with hot puris and raita for a simple soul satisfying meal.

Curry Potatoes

Ingredients: (Serves 4)

- 1 peeled and cut medium-sized potato
- 1 chopped medium-sized onion
- 3 cloves of minced garlic
- 1 tsp. of garam masala
- 2 tbsp. oil

- 2 cups of water
- Salt and pepper to desired taste

Method:

1. In a heavy pot, heat the oil and add onion and garlic and sauté till soft, do not brown.
2. Add potatoes and stir for about 1 minute.
3. Add water and continue cooking until the curry gets thickened and potatoes cooked.
4. Add garam masala, salt and pepper. Adjust to desired level of seasoning.

This recipe from Shirley Ramratan, who migrated to Canada from Trinidad in 1974 is rather interesting and has as a amazing story.. Her great grandmother was from Bihar who passed on this favourite dish to the family. We are fascinated by how it thrives on even after 4 generations far away from its country of origin. Somewhere in time, the tomato or cumin seeds, coriander powder, green coriander, that many generally use for this dish, skipped a generation, but the dish lives on. The closest original recipe for this dish can be found under the aloo Rassa recipe in this cookbook. Sometimes Shirley says she adds eggplant to this dish.

Vadi (Dried daal)

Ingredients:

- 3 kg split black urad dal
- 2 kg white urad dal
- 6 tbs. green chillies, ground
- ¼ cup ground ginger
- ½ cup cumin seeds
- ¼ cup pepper corns coarsely ground
- ¼ cup cloves
- 1/8 cup cinnamon
- ¼ cup black cardamom
- ¼ cup whole coriander coarsely ground
- 3 tbs. pumpkin seeds
- 1 small green pumpkin
- a pinch of asafoetida (Hing)
- Ginger Powder
- Water
- 2 ½ tbsp. salt

Method:

1. Soak black urad dal overnight and then rub to take the softened skin out. Soak the white urad dal overnight as well. Mix both dals and grind in blender till coarsely ground.
2. In a large bowl, add to the ground dal's the ground green chillies, ground ginger, whole cumin seeds, roughly ground peppercorns, ground cloves, ground cinnamon, ground black cardamom, ground coriander, roughly broken pumpkin seeds and salt.
3. Mix very well by hands, whipping it and pounding the mix to combine very well. Do not use any electric help or whisk as the texture will change and not be coarse as needed for the Vadi.
4. In another bowl, dissolve a pinch of asafoetida (hing) and ¼ tbs. ginger powder in ½ cup water.
5. Wet hands and drop 2inch size balls of mixture onto cookie trays or a tin sheet.
6. Find a very sunny spot to put the Vadis to dry.
7. On the second day, turn the bottom surface up to help dry them in the sun, on the third day turn them again till all surfaces are exposed to the sun and fully dry. It must be completely dry, otherwise the inside will grow mould and ruin this laborious product.
8. This can be kept for over a year in an air tight container. Roast required quantity in a little bit oil or ghee until slightly red. Can be used in a number of curries, mutter paneer or rice pulao dishes.

Mrs. Jagdeesh Kaur's eyes were glowing with fond memories of sunny Africa, where as a young girl she so enjoyed seeing her mom and other ladies making Vadis. It took us a while to understand the drying process; there they used to put the Vadis on large tin sheets to dry them on the thatched roof tops. She suggests for us here, in Canada, to put the cookie trays on the hot cement of our patio's to help speed the drying process. Even though the quantity of ingredients seems large, they last a long time and need not to be prepared for over a year. Many of our seniors here miss this old fashioned, healthy and nutritious item because the store bought ones not only lack real taste and flavor, but also the loving hands that used to make them.

Channna

Ingredients: (Serves 6-8)

- 2 lbs channa white
- 1 onion – medium, ground to paste
- 1 garlic – small pod, ground to paste
- 2 ginger pieces – chopped
- 3 tsp. anardana powder
- 1 tomato – medium, chopped
- 1 onion – cut into thin rings (for garnish)
- 4 tbsp of chopped fresh coriander leaves
- **Masala:**
- 2 tsp cumin seeds
- 4 black cardamoms
- 1½ cinnamon stick
- 4 cloves
- 2 tsp whole coriander

Method:

1. Soak the channa in water for a few hours.
2. Boil in water with ½ tsp of salt.
3. Cook till done (not mushy)
4. In another pot, heat a few tbsp of oil.
5. Brown the onion paste a few moments, add garlic and ginger to pot.
6. Add the boiled channa and bring to a boil.
7. Add the masala and cook to desired thickness.
8. Add the anardana and salt to taste.
9. Serve topped with the tomatoes, onions and coriander.

Usha Sharma lived in the state of Kashmir and migrated in 1978 to Canada. A dedicated volunteer to date in the community, she's made these channa amongst other dishes for years to the enjoyment of many.

Baingan Bharta

Ingredients: (Serves 2-4)

- 1 large eggplant, roasted and made into pulp
- 2 red onions chopped
- 1 fresh medium tomato chopped
- 4 tbs. oil
- 1 piece grated ginger
- ½ cup peas
- 1 tbsp. garam masala
- handful of green coriander
- a few green chopped chillies
- Salt to taste

Method:

1. Heat oil in the pan, cook chopped onions and ginger till slightly browned.
2. Add peas, eggplant pulp and tomato and roast till the oil leaves the side of the pan.
3. Add garam masala, chopped green coriander and chillies. Adjust salt to taste.

Sarla Bhatla came to Canada in 1971. Her simple recipe of this very popular dish is amazing and tastes like the one made back home. She suggests to put in her homemade garam masala. Perfected for over 20 years, she grinds together 1lb coriander seeds, a fistful of cloves, 20 black cardamoms, a fistful of black pepper corns with ½ lb of cumin seeds .This yields her famous garam masala which she recommends to use to help one with a cold and cough. Please experiment with the cloves and peppers to suite the taste.

Lauki Yakhni

Ingredients: (Serves 4)

- 1 medium-sized lauki
- 4 tbsp. of vegetable oil
- Pinch of hing
- ½ tbsp. cumin seeds
- 1 tsp. turmeric powder
- 1 tsp. chili powder
- 1 tsp. ginger powder
- 1 tsp. fennel powder
- 1 tsp. coriander powder
- 1 tsp. garam masala
- 4 tbsp. whipped dahi (yoghurt)
- Water to mix
- Salt to desired taste
- Green coriander to garnish

Method:

1. Peel and cut lauki into ½ inch pieces.
2. Heat oil in a kadhai or pot. Add cumin seeds and hing. When oil sputters, add turmeric, red chillis and lauki.
3. Stir and add salt, ginger, fennel seeds, coriander powder and cover the pan. Let the mixture simmer until the lauki is tender.
4. Add the whipped yogurt with some water according to desired gravy thickness and simmer for 5 minutes.
5. Add garam masala and chopped green coriander.
6. Serve hot with boiled rice or rotis.

Ranjana Kaul came to Montreal in the early 90's and is a very active community volunteer. Her recipe has the flavour of fennel seed (saunf), a typical spice largely used in her province of origin, Kashmir – the land known for its abundance in natural beauty.

Besan Gatta Curry

Ingredients: (Serves 4)

- **Ingredients for Gattas:**
- 200 gms besan
- 1 tsp. garam masala (preferably MDH brand)
- 1 tbsp. oil
- ½ tsp. salt
- Boiling water
-
- Ingredients for curry:
- 1 tbsp. oil
- 1 onion medium -chopped
- 2 tsp. ginger - chopped
- 1 tsp. red chilli
- 250 gram yoghurt
- 1 tsp. turmeric
- The boiled Gatta water

Method:

1. Mix the besan, garam masala, oil and salt with some water to make a stiff dough.
2. Make 5-6 thin and long strips of dough, like thin hot dogs.
3. Put these strips in boiling water and cook 6-7 minutes.
4. Cut the strips into small pieces after taking out from the water.
5. Keep the water for the curry.
6. In another pot, heat oil and cook onions until they are soft. Add ginger and cook for 1 minute.
7. In a bowl, add the red chilies and turmeric to the yoghurt and mix well.
8. Add the gatta pieces to mixture in bowl and then add all this to the onion and ginger cooking in the pot. Keep stirring the mixture until it boils.
9. Adjust the gravy on a regular basis by using the left over water from step 5.
10. Serve with rice or roti.

Mrs. Uma Grover moved from Pakistan at the young age of 2 years. She has a Pathani origin and has lived in Palampur before migrating to Canada. The details she added to this Rajashtani dish combined with the idea of keeping it simple, yields a great result which one can so easily enjoy here.

BREADS

To many seniors, food is a way of living. It is the substance consumed to provide nutrition that supports the body and our seniors keep insisting to keep it fresh by daily cooking. To see cooked food from a couple of days before is hard for them to accept, yet they have adapted to this change. Given a choice, in their hearts they would rather have one simple dal with fresh rotis than have many previously cooked dishes with store purchased rotis.

It is common to hear adults and seniors alike often say 'duo roti kay luja kaam karthey hai' meaning one earns to bring bread home. South Asians use a variety of flour for their flat bread from white flour for naans to buckwheat, gram, waterchestnut with whole wheat being the most popular.

Aloo Parantha

Ingredients: (Makes 4)

- **For Filling:**
  - 2 large potatoes - boiled and mashed
  - 1 green chilli - chopped
  - 3 tbsp. green coriander leaves - chopped
  - ½ tsp. pomegranate seeds - ground
  - ¼ tsp. garam masala
  - Salt to desired taste

- **For Dough:**
  - 1 cup wheat flour (atta)
  - Enough warm milk to make dough
  - ¼ cup wheat flour - for dusting
  - 1 tbsp. ghee/butter/oil
  - 3 tbsp. oil for frying

Method:

1. Mix all filling ingredients and keep aside.
2. Make a medium soft dough with the wheat flour and warm milk.
3. Knead dough well with ghee on hands and keep aside covered with damp cloth for ½ hour. If you are new to making paranthas, make a firmer dough, it is easier to control the rolling process.
4. Break 1 ½ inch round dough piece and roll into a round ball.
5. Press dough into dry flour with fingers and use rolling pin to create into a 4" diameter flat disc.
6. Use twice the amount of dough for filling, placing into the centre of the disc and fold the sides up and on top to cover the filling.
7. Press the filled dough into dry flour and then use a rolling pin to flatten.
8. Put flattened dough onto a heated tava. Brown one side, flip to cover with oil and turn over. Cook both sides until nicely brown.

Asha Arya finds by kneading the atta with milk, her paranthas turn out softer and have a more delicate flavour. Anardana gives q tangy kick and keeps the filling drier to work better with than lemon juice. Over 70 years old, she enjoys making this family favourite with lots of pleasure. She loves to knit.

Dal Puri

Ingredients: (Makes 4)

- **For Dal filling:**
  - 1 cup channa or mutter dal
  - ¼ tsp. turmeric powder
  - ¼ tsp. cumin powder
  - ¼ tsp. red chili- powder
  - ¼ tsp. whole cumin
  - Salt to desired taste

- **For Puri:**
  - 2 cups of all-purpose flour
  - Warm water
  - Oil for kneading
  - flour for dusting

Method:

1. Wash and soak dal for 5 hours. Boil with turmeric and salt till done. Mash dal between fingertips to check and see if it is ready - soft yet firm on inside.
2. Drain dal and cool.
3. Grind dal coarsely and mix remaining ingredients.
4. To make dough, knead flour with warm water. Coat palms with oil and knead well. Keep covered aside for ½ hour with a damp cloth.
5. Divide dough into equal round portions.
6. Take a dough ball, press to make a depression and fill with dal mixture (1 portion of dal for 2 portions of dough) OR roll dough into 4" diameter circles and put dal in the middle.
7. Fold up dough circle to cover the dal filling. Roll into a ball and press to coat with dry flour. Rolling the stuffed dough thin to make a circle about 10" in diameter by using a rolling pin. Be careful not to let the dal spill out from the dough.
8. On medium-high tawa, cook one side of the dal puri and flip to cook the other side.
9. Put on ghee or butter before serving.

Mrs. Krishna Choudry Varma recalls this regional preparation being made in 1940 by her mom. It was given as a morning offering to the cow. It was also a must during festivals and special occasions often enjoyed with kheer or a korma. From Faizabad in Uttar Pradesh, this stuffed flatbread has delighted many here in Montreal since 1975 by her hands. The popularity of this Dal puri has extended itself from the Asian subcontinent to Guyana, Trinidad and the Caribbean, even though it is very intensive labour.

Farida Ali well known for making these as well is very pleased with this preparation. This is a complete meal since it contains both protein and carbohydrate. With mango pickle or chutney rolled up inside this becomes a good food to travel with she suggests. With airlines cutting down on food services she packs this for family members knowing they will be satisfied.

Bhatura

Ingredients: (Makes 12)

- 3 cups maida (all-purpose flour)
- ½ cup whole wheat flour
- 1/4 cup sooji (semolina)
- 2 tsp. salt
- 1 tsp. ajwain
- 1 tsp. leveled baking powder

- 2 tsp. dry yeast + 1 teaspoon sugar
- ½ cup milk
- 1 tbsp. oil
- Warm water
- Oil for deep frying

Method:

1. Mix all dry ingredients in a bowl.
2. Add warm milk to dry mix and add warm water to make a stiff dough. Keep covered with damp cloth for 15 minutes.
3. Oil palms and knead dough very well. Cover and keep to rise for 2 ½ hours in a warm place (i.e. oven or top of fridge).
4. Once raised, punch down the dough and make equal sized balls. Round each and flatten into 5-inch circles with rolling pin. Deep fry in hot oil and press down to puff the bhatura. Brown the bhatura on both sides and serve hot

Rajni Khanna is an amazing cook. Her bhatura's are a hit and enjoyed by other seniors and children. She mastered this recipe by repeating it multiple times over many years and adjusting to see the dough rise according to the change of temperature. Climate being very different in Quebec here from Punjab. She says the ajwain gives a good flavor and milk makes the bhatura soft. A classic way to enjoy these is with a side of Channa (Chole)

Muli Parantha

Ingredients: (Makes 6)

- **For Filling:**
- 1 white radish – medium, grated
- ½ onion – medium- finely chopped
- 1 tsp ginger – finely chopped
- 3 green chilies, finely chopped
- 2 tbsp green coriander, finely chopped
- 1 tsp. anardana powder
- ¼ tsp. amchur

- 1 tsp cumin seeds
- ½ tsp. ajwain
- Salt and red chilies to taste
- **For Dough:**
- 2 cups whole wheat flour
- ¾ cup luke warm water
- flour for dusting
- Oil

Method:

1. Drain water out of grated muli and mix all ingredients, except salt and red chilies. Keep aside.
2. Make a semi stiff dough with the wheat flour and water. Knead using some oil on palm of hand. Knead and let sit for ½ hour in fridge.
3. When ready to prepare, mix the salt and red chilies with the filling mix. By not adding them before, the filling will not soften and the muli will retain its water.
4. Make 2 round balls between the palm of your hands and press each in the atta, covering both sides.
5. With a rolling pin, roll the 2 dough balls to 4" circles.
6. In the center of one of the circles, add 2 tbsp. of filling. Top with the other circle and press the bottom and top edge of dough firmly together.
7. Keeping the filling between them, coat with dry flour on both sides and roll out till evenly thinned (about 8 inches in diameter).
8. Apply a small amount of oil on a hot pan and cook the bottom surface of the parantha until golden brown. Flip over and cook the other side until golden brown. You can also cook the stuffed bread without oil to make 'muli ki roti' (a healthier choice) instead of 'muli ka parantha'.

This recipe is a family favorite of Mohin Preet Kaur, affectionately called Mimi. Born in Lahore and raised in India, she has enjoyed making these amazing paranthas for over 35 years in her home in the South Shore and is a community worker.

Chicken Parantha

Ingredients: (Makes 6-8)

- 1 kg. of boneless chicken breast cut into 4 pieces
- 1 tsp. of ground cumin powder
- 1 cup plain yoghurt
- 3 tsp. oil
- 1 tsp. red chili powder
- 2 tbsp. of kastoori methi
- 1 onion medium-chopped
- 1 tsp. lime juice
- 2 tsp. crushed chilies
- 1 tsp. ginger paste

- 2 cloves of garlic paste
- 2 tbsp. of chopped fresh coriander
- Salt and pepper to desired taste
-

For Dough:
- 2 cups whole wheat flour
- ¾ cup lukewarm water
- Dry flour for dusting
- Oil

Method:

1. Marinate chicken in yoghurt, oil, salt, red chili powder and cumin powder for at least 6 hours.
2. Bake chicken in marinade at 425°F for 45 minutes.
3. Let the chicken cool and grind it in blender.
4. Mix garlic, ginger, onion, lime juice and salt with the chicken.
5. Add crushed chilies and fresh coriander to baked chicken mix.
6. Mix all very well and keep aside.
7. Make a semi-stiff dough with the wheat flour and water. Knead using some oil in the palm of hands. Knead and let sit for ½ hour in fridge.
8. When ready, make 2 round balls between palm of your hands and press into the atta.
9. With a rolling pin, roll each dough ball into 4 inch circles.
10. In the center of one circle, put 2 tbsp of filling. Top with the other circle and press the bottom and top edge of dough firmly together.
11. Coat with dry flour on both side and roll out the paranthas till evenly thinned (about 8 inches in diameter).
12. Fry one side of the parantha on hot tava with a small amount of oil. When the bottom is golden brown, flip to the other side and cook until it's golden brown.

Amita Khanna says this was a super hit item for youngsters and though this recipe seems like work it is really worth making again and again…

Methi (Fenugreek) Parantha

Ingredients: (Makes 6)

- 500 gms. whole wheat flour
- 200 gms. methi leaves
- 150 ml cooking oil
- 1 tbsp. cumin seeds

- ½ tbsp.turmeric powder
- ½ tbsp. garam masala powder
- ½ tbsp. red chili powder
- Salt to desired taste

Method:

1. Wash and dry methi leaves and chop them to small pieces.
2. Mix wheat flour, methi leaves, oil, garam masala, turmeric powder, red chilli powder and cumin seeds in a bowl. Sprinkle on salt to taste and mix well.
3. Add a small amount of water. Knead the mixture. You may require more water to smooth the dough. Knead dough until it becomes soft.
4. Allow dough to settle for ½ hour.
5. Divide dough into lemon-sized balls.
6. Roll each ball and add dry flour to improve rolling. Make uniform circular discs (6 inches in diameter and 6 to 7 mm thick).
7. Fold the disc into half twice (will look like a quarter disc) and roll again into a triangular shape. Repeat once or twice.
8. Heat tawa (without oil) and add a parantha, cooking each well. Heat each side for several minutes and keep flipping. Air bubbles that appear will make your paranthas fluffy and soft.
9. Once all have been cooked, add oil on the surface of the tawa and fry the parantha until it becomes golden brown.
10. Serve with your favorite side dish or subji.

Many seniors put the methi in the dough and make it into a roti to avoid frying with oil for health reasons. A complete meal with dahi and achar.

Roti

Ingredients: (Makes 10-12)

- 2 cups whole wheat flour (Chapati/atta flour)
- 3/4 cup warm water
- Clarified butter or Ghee
- flour for dusting

Method:

1. Use a large mixing bowl and add the whole wheat flour..
2. Add warm water, a little at a time, to form a medium soft dough. Do not overwork the dough
3. Cover with damp cloth and let it rest for 15 minutes.
4. Heat tawa or skillet on medium heat.
5. Knead the dough once and divide into golf ball size balls.
6. Dip onc ball into the flour to coat and roll it out into a thin disc. Keep dipping the roti into the dry flour to prevent it from sticking to the rolling surface.
7. Shake or rub off excess flour from the roti and place it onto the hot tawa.
8. Flip to the other side once you see bubbles appear on the surface. Allow it to cook for 10- 15 seconds.
9. Increase the stove heat to high, gently pick the roti up with tongs, remove the tawa off of the flame, flip the roti over and place onto an open flame.
10. The roti should puff up with air. Flip it over and cook on the other side.
11. Place the cooked roti into an insulated container and smear with Ghee or clarified butter and repeat the process for the remaining dough.

Roti is the most common household bread to accompany south-Indian foods. Many stories fables songs jokes revolve around the roti. Staple food for substance many seniors consider this the main reason for which one goes to work to be able to earn to feed the family its bread. Simple put a person needs "roti kapra aur makan" (meaning bread, clothing, and a roof on top of the head) to take care of the body's physical needs.

RICE

To many seniors, food is a way of living. It is the substance consumed to provide nutrition that supports the body and our seniors keep insisting to keep it fresh by daily cooking. To see cooked food from a couple of days before is hard for them to accept, yet they have adapted to this change. Given a choice, in their hearts they would rather have one simple dal with fresh rotis than have many previously cooked dishes with store purchased rotis. A senior recounted of having to move to India from Pakistan way before partition. Her father travelled between the two places due to his work. Once partition began, the family realized it would be impossible for him to return home. Not knowing his whereabouts and then to see him standing in front of their very eyes, one day, was truly a miracle. To this day she often finds herself thanking that unknown kind gentleman who took her father by hand, gave him an air ticket to India saying "no matter where the plane lands in India at least you will be safe." Like her, many seniors feel that one should proceed in life doing random acts of kindness and spreading them far and wide – much like grains of rice.

Rice, in many South Asian homes is not only for nourishment but is very symbolic for spiritual growth. Often seen on tilaks or thrown joyfully at wedding ceremonies, it has become a sign of prosperity, abundance and growth. Its white color is considered as a sign of purity. It is grown in many varieties, both short or long grains and "basmati", is popular for its fragrance.

Yakhni Pulao

Ingredients: (Makes 8)

- 1 kg. of boned chicken or mutton
- 2 cups of washed rice
- 1 large onion - chopped
- 1 ½" piece ginger
- 5 tbsp. yoghurt

- **Spices:**
- 3 tsp. saunf
- 3 tsp. whole cumin seeds
- 3 tsp. whole coriander seeds
- 2 green cardamom
- 4 cloves
- 1 tsp. peppercorns

Method:

1. Mix spices and tie them in a cheese cloth. Add this spice bundle, with cheese cloth, into a pressure cooker.
2. Add 4 cups of water in pressure cooker with meat (or you can cook open over stove) till meat is firm. Take meat out from the broth.
3. In a pot, fry onion in oil, add the meat and cook till it turns brown. Add grated ginger and yoghurt and then add the rice and salt. Add broth and bring to boil. Put the heat on low, cover and cook for 15min. Keep lid on, remove after 10 minutes. Stir.

Suriya Saeed has been in Montreal since the seventies and is well known for making delicious foods. This grandmother loves poetry and helps others be it by her cooking skills, support or knowledge esp. in Urdu amongst many other talents.

Biryani

Ingredients: (Serves 6-8)

- 4 cups of basmati rice
- 1/2 kg meat of your choice. Cut into small pieces and washed.
- 1 large onion, finely chopped
- 6-7 cloves of garlic
- 2" of fresh Ginger
- 2-3 green cardamom
- 2 big cardamoms
- 5 cloves
- 2 inch long cinnamon stick
- 1/2 tsp of black pepper

- 2 bay leaves
- 1 cup of plain yoghurt
- 1 1/2 cup of oil
- 1 cup water
- 3 liters of water
- Salt to taste

Method:

For The Meat:

1. Heat oil and fry onions till lightly browned. Remove onions from oil.
2. In the same oil, add the ginger garlic paste, meat and all herbs and spices (except green cardamom).
3. Cook until there is no more water in the meat.
4. Mix yoghurt with 1 cup of water, add it to the meat. Cook till the meat is tender and fully cooked.
5. Make sure all water is evaporated from the meat.

For The Rice:

1. Wash rice and keep aside.
2. In another pot heat the 1\2 cup oil.
3. Add in the 2-3 green cardamom.
4. Add the 3 liters of water and boil.
5. Add the rice to the boiling water and cook till almost done.
6. Drain the water from the rice.
7. Gently layer the rice and meat using a ladle.
8. Simmer on low heat for about half an hour or till rice is fully cooked.
9. If rice is not cooked sprinkle some water and cook for a few more minutes.
10. When ready, garnish with the fried onions, food coloring and saffron.

Over the years Nighat Khan has become a kitchen wizard. Both her children and her husband sing praises of her cooking, as do many friends and relatives. She fondly recalls enjoying vegetarian food .Her story of how during Diwali celebrations in India, her Hindu neighbors would put diyas (lights) on the walls of her family garden. This really warms our hearts. She longs for those moments of her neighborhood which were once so pure, real and were all felt togetherness.

CHUTNEY

Imagine the joy seniors feel in preparing special recipes for their families and see them relish their made dish - somehow this is far more satisfying than eating the food themselves. We witnessed a senior hold up a tomato in his hand, saying it does not taste like the organic tomato from his gardens in the old country, nevertheless, improvising and fine tuning many techniques by trial and error, and not giving up until he found a method to replicate the taste of a chutney he once knew.

In another story, a hardworking, caring departed senior's last handmade chutney bottle in the fridge became a treasure to his family. To see his daughter make it now days, like he did, keeps him close to family and friends. To make good chutney is no joke and many take making it very seriously. It can bring out the food flavors for maximum enjoyments and aid in digestion.

Bengali Tomato Chutney

Ingredients: (Serves 6)

- 2 cups tomatoes - cut in long cubes
- ¼ tsp. panchphoran (saunf, zeera, rye, methi, kalonji) seed
- 1 tbsp. raisins
- ½ tsp. ginger - cut into thin strips
- 1 tsp. green chilies - chopped
- 1 tbsp. sugar
- 1 tsp. mustard oil
- Salt to desired taste

Method:

1. Heat oil in a pot and add panchphoran seeds. Cook for 1 minute.
2. Add tomatoes and salt and mix well. Cover and heat for 3 minutes.
3. Add raisins, ginger, green chilies and sugar, and cook for 8 to 10 minutes.
4. Cool and refrigerate in an air tight box.

Mr. Devinder Dev Kaushal's tomato chutney is so tasty that it goes so well with rice, parathas or roti. Accompanies many dishes very well. Enjoy!

Green Chili Accompaniment

Ingredients: (Serves 4-6)

- ½ cup green chilies - ground
- ½ lemon
- 2 tsp. of oil
- Pinch of sugar
- Salt to desired taste

Method:

1. In heated oil, add green chilies and stir until water dries.
2. Add the rest of the ingredients and adjust to taste.

This preparation is used as an accompaniment to many meals. Jagdish Kaur says Punjabis really enjoy their food red hot with spicy green chilies. However, with changes in diet and different tastes, she finds this chutney allows for those seeking their fiery urge to be quenched easily, by having this on the side than having to mix the green chilies in the whole dish.

Red Garlic Accompaniment

Ingredients: (Serves 2-4)

- 1 whole garlic
- 6 red chillies
- A pinch of hing
- Olive oil
- Salt to desired taste

Method:

1. Peel garlic and blend with all ingredients in a small food processer.
2. Thin with water to desired consistency.
3. Serve over ragda patties or with dosa.

Malika Gandhi has seen this preparation in Gujarat, made from fresh dried red chillies. She suggests keeping it in an air-tight bottle.

Kerala Ridge Gourd Chutney

Ingredients: (Serves 6)

- 1 large ridge gourd (peerkangailauki)
- ½ cup dry urad dal
- ¼ cup dry channa dal
- oil

- 6 red chillis
- A pinch of hing
- 1 tbsp. tamarind (imili)
- Salt to desired taste

Method:

1. Peel the gourd and cut in pieces and coat with oil. Fry in pan to make the pieces soft.
2. Add urad and channa dals and fry on low heat till they are red.
3. Add red chillies and roast as well.
4. Coarsely grind all these in blender and mix in salt, hing and tamarind.
5. Add some water to thin the chutney as the dals rise and thicken the chutney.
6. Enjoy this with dosa or idli or chapattis.

Prema Vengopalan is happy this gourd is readily available here now in Indo-Canadian grocery stores. She is careful to peel the sharp skin of the gourd. Her family enjoys this chutney with this south Indian food.

Imli (Tamarind) Chutney

Ingredients: (Serves 6)

- ¼ cup of tamarind paste
- ¼ cup of jaggery ("gur" in hindi)
- 1 ½ cup water
- ½ tsp. chilli powder
- ½ teaspoon ajwine or cumin seeds
- 1 tsp. oil
- Kala namak to desired taste
- Salt to desired taste

Method:

1. Thin the tamarind paste in the water and keep aside for ½ hour.
2. In hot oil add the cumin or ajwine seeds. When the sputtering stops pour this into the tamarind water mix. Boil this overall mixture.
3. Add the remaining ingredients and boil the mixture for a few minutes.
4. Adjust the sweetness to taste.
5. Can add whole red chillies/dates/raisins/coconut/almonds etc. if you desire.

This , a sweet and tangy chutney can be made spicy by the addition of extra chilies or made rich by adding dates, raisons, almonds, and coconut. Goes t great on dhai varas or in chaat preparations.

DRINKS

One thing we realized is how receptive seniors are to have visitors - and what gracious hosts they are, easily sharing their life stories. How quickly we are offered something to drink as we sat, was a common observation. From ripples of laughter, to silence, deep conversations and the occasional teary eyes - those of us who were privileged to gather this information for the cookbook relished in silence seeing the passing on of the baton, or rather, the passing of these bailans (bailan means rolling pin in hindi). Revisiting old recipes and seeing their new infusion forms; from past homes to their newer ones …. this was to witness a migration in itself.

Fast foods, home foods, comfort foods, and soul foods showed us the intimate link and relationship our seniors have built with food. It helps aid them through sickness or rise higher in spiritual health. A "garam chai ka pyala" (hot cup of tea) is a ritual that many times really has nothing to do with drinking the tea. The comfort to share the warmth, sweetness with company and chit chat somehow makes chai the excuse .The point is to be in company and connect. Our elders feel that to offer an unknown person a drink of water is the best deed a human can perform. One has be responsible for physical as well as spiritual growth, that is why to give someone water becomes a, "punya ka kaam"(a work done unselfishly acknowledged as a good deed). Even today by bus stops one can see a person offering water to travelers in South Asia.

Masala Chai

Ingredients: (Serves 4)

- 4 crushed green Cardamom
- Pinch of cinnamon powder
- 2 cloves
- ¼ inch piece of fresh ginger
- 3 tea sachets of black tea
- 2 cups milk
- 4 tbs sugar
- 3 cups water

Method:

1. Put 3 cups of water to boil.
2. Add the first five ingredients and bring the water to boil again.
3. Cover and simmer for 6-8 minutes on very low heat.
4. Add sugar, milk and simmer on medium heat.
5. Strain into four cups and serve.

Mango Lassi

Ingredients: (Serves 2)

- 1 cup of plain yogurt
- ½ cup of fresh mango or mango pulp
- 1 cup of crushed ice
- 3 tsp. of sugar

Method:

1. Blend all ingredients. You can add some water if lassi seems thick.
2. Serve chilled or keep in fridge till consumed. Summer and a glass of Mango Lassi will go very well together.

Chai

Ingredients: (Serves 2)

- 1 cup milk
- 11/2 cup water
- 2 tsp. sugar
- 2 tsp. loose black tea leaves

Method:

1. In a clean pot boil milk water and sugar together
2. Reduce heat to low, add tea leaves.
3. Cover and let simmer 3-4 minutes
4. Strain with sieve and serve tea hot.

Mr. Gurcharan Singh Bhatia is an 80-year-old plus young at heart man who really knows his tea. Simple as it may be to make, yet it is an art. He insists a pot previously used will alter the taste of the tea if not cleaned well. The choice of tea leaves are many, but in Canada, he recommends using a mix of dried orange pekoe, yellow label and Darjeeling tea. He believes that for a good taste – tea must have not only body, flavour and colour but texture as well. He suggests adding a pinch of Darjeeling tea to the boiling liquids for flavour. According to him, over the years the quality of the leaves has changed. He loved to bring his tea leaves from India but now finds tea quality has greatly been compromised everywhere.

Meethi Lassi

Ingredients: (Serves 2)

- 1 cup of yoghurt
- ½ cup of water
- ½ cup of ice cubes
- 3 to 5 tsp. of sugar
- A pinch of salt
- A dollop of plain yoghurt

Method:

1. Blend on high speed in a blender all the ingredients, except the last.
2. Stop when it is frothy and pour into 2 or 3 glasses.
3. Adjust the sweetness to your desired taste. Top it with a dollop of fresh yoghurt for garnish. Enjoy.

Pineapple Lassi

2)

- 1 cup of fresh pineapple pieces
- ½ cup of plain yoghurt
- ½ cup of water
- 2 tbs of sugar
- ½ cup of ice cube

Method:

1. Blend all ingredients in the blender till smooth and serve immediately!
2. Bananas should be very ripe to give this lassi its flavor and color.

Namkeen Lassi

Ingredients: (Serves 2)

- 1 cup of plain yoghurt
- 1 tsp. roasted cumin seeds
- 1 cup of cold milk
- 1 tsp. of lemon juice
- ½ cup of ice cube

- Salt to taste
- Red chilli to taste

Method:

1. Blend all the ingredients and serve. Can add mint leaves as well.
2. In hot weather this homemade cooling drink has many variations and is made in most parts of India. Banana, nuts, peaches, strawberries, orange and vanilla lassi are newer flavours. For more food value, many use chilled milk instead of water to thin the lassi.

A very interesting Hindu mythology tale revolved about the Gods and demons not having immortality and asked Lord Vishnu to change this. In turn he told them how together they could make the elixir of immortality, called Amrit.

Ajanta, the cosmic snake, was wrapped around Mt Meru, the cosmic mountain. The Gods from one side and the demons on the other then churned the mountain into the cosmic sea to bring forth the sweet amrit which they drank to become immortal. During this, Lord Vishnu had converted himself into a gigantic tortoise to provide a solid foundation for the mountain. It is said that after this process, an endless variety of drinks appeared; Tea, Coffee, Lassi, Nimbu Pani, Fruit juices instead of just water.

Nimbu Pani

Ingredients: (Serves 2)

- 2 Lemons or Limes
- 2 tsp. of sugar
- ½ tsp. of salt
- 1 ½ cup of cold water
- ½ cup of ice

Method:

1. Mix the juice from the lemons or limes with the sugar, salt and water.
2. Stir still the sugar and salt till it dissolves.
3. Add ice and serve.
4. Nimbu Pani can be made in a 'salty' version by omitting the sugar content and stirring with a pinch of black salt.

MISCELLANEOUS IMPORTANT RECIPES

Full of wisdom, our seniors love to impart knowledge and are readily available to speak their minds, giving advice. Most seniors emphasized to never underestimate the power of a good laugh – that life is easier with a good sense of humor. Their simple message is to find 'tasalee' (loosely meaning finding satisfaction, calm and contentment) in everything that one does.

Haldi Cure

Ingredients:
- ½ lb. of fresh haldi
- ½ lb. of whole wheat flour
- ½ lb. of sugar
- ½ lb. of ghee

Method:
1. Peel and finely grate the fresh haldi.
2. In a pot, over medium-low heat, melt 1/4 lb. of ghee and roast the haldi until the liquid dries up.
3. In another pot melt the other 1/4 lb. of ghee and over medium-low heat and roast the whole wheat flour.
4. Cool both pots and mix ingredients from both pots together well.
5. Eat a laddu-sized amount of haldi each day.

Mrs. Indravati Sharma came to Canada in 1977 from Jalandhar and today she nears ninety years. She cannot stop singing praises of haldi. For years, she has recommended haldi to many, to even simply having it in hot mil to ease body aches. It can be consumed even to help cure a cold. Having faced many health issues including numerous surgeries and pain, she credits haldi as a cure-all and the reason why at this wise age she is so remarkably fit. This is an age old cure tested by faith and belief. It gives good results and is still made in many villages as a medical aid to help inflammation.

Dahi

Ingredients:
- 4 cups Whole Milk
- 1 tbsp. starter Yoghurt (or room temperature yogurt)

Method:
1. Bring milk to boil on the stovetop or microwave
2. Allow milk to cool to slightly warmer than lukewarm
3. Add starter yoghurt to the milk and blend together with a hand blender or whisk.
4. Transfer milk to a heat proof container with a tight fitting lid.
5. Preheat oven to 180 degrees F and switch oven OFF.
6. Place container with milk into the warm oven and set timer for 3 1\2 hours.
7. After 3 1\2 hours, remove yoghurt from oven and store in refrigerator

Tips:
1. Starter yoghurt can be from your previous batch or you can buy a small single serve plain yoghurt from the grocery store.
2. Do not add starter yoghurt into hot milk or yoghurt as the bacteria will die and the yoghurt will not set.
3. If you prefer yoghurt which is on the tart (sour) side, keep the yoghurt in the warm oven for 5-6 hours. The longer you keep it outside, the more sour it becomes. This is great for making kadhi.

Desi Ghee

Ingredients:
- 1 lb. unsalted butter (Lactantia brand gives great results)

Method:
1. In a heavy bottom pan melt the butter over low-heat so that it does not brown at all.
2. Bring to a simmer by increasing heat to medium and the foam bubbles. Stir once.
3. Lower the heat and watch the simmering process until the milk solids settle to the bottom on the pan and the transparent butter is afloat.
4. Drain into another container without disturbing the sediments. Once the ghee cools, it will solidify and can be kept at room temperature.

Desi Ghee is made commonly is most households. Even to date, many rub this onto their palms and skin as a moisturizer or help soothe a burn. Since it has medical properties, though it is high in fat, it is highly popular. Ghee is mainly used to butter rotis and cook parathans or in food tampering.

Paneer

Ingredients:

* 8 cups of whole milk
* ¼ cup of lemon juice
* ½ cup water

Method:

1. Mix lemon juice in hot water and keep aside.
2. Bring to boil whole milk and stir to prevent it sticking the bottom.
3. Once milk boils, gradually add lemon juice mixture
4. The curd will separate from whey. Turn of heat.
5. Drain in solids in cheese cloth
6. Wrap cloth and rinse and squeeze well.
7. Even out the paneer and place under a heavy pan for about an hour
8. Rinse when set. By washing, the excess lemon juice flavour is removed.

Many South Asians separate the paneer by using yoghurt or vinegar. Many use the whey to make a good curry or to gundo atta "kneading the dough".

COMMENTS FROM OUR YOUTH

During the course of making this book, seniors began sharing their stories and recipes with the youth. Aangan began hosting events involving the youth and getting feedback about the items being prepared.

We were amazed at how the youth relished the different types of foods they sampled and prepared. Following are some of the comments they voiced or wrote to us.

Zucchini Squares

- Tastes amazing with the green chutney.

- Delicious. Moist, light, a bit like quiche.

- Good, very moist. Good chutney.

Punjabi Kadhi

- Punjabi Kadhi was good with the Dal - roti. They complement one another.

- No two kadhi's taste the same. Everyone cooks it differently even if they are cooked with the same recipe. It always comes out differently and uniquely in taste.

Zucchini Soup

- Amazing.

- Can't wait to get the book to see this recipe!

- Light.

Tuk

- Delicious.

- Can't wait to try to make it at home.

Yakhni Pulao

- Yummy taste in the rice.

- Moist flavor for chicken.

- Delicious.

- Simple and tasty.

Lamb Curry

- Delicious.

- How come ours at home doesn't taste like this!

- Lots of spice and flavors.

- Tastes better with naan than rice.

Sweet Lassi

- Refreshing.

- So easy to make at home.

- Light, is like yop.

- I like to have yoghurt this way.

Gajar Halwa

- Yummy & delicious.
- A nice way to eat your carrots.
- I like the long way of cooking it.

Masala Corn

- So simple and tasty.
- Really delicious.
- We will surely make it in the house.
- Never thought of making corn this way.

Nimbu pani

- Hint of salt tastes nice in it.
- Right amount for sweetness.
- Real refreshing. Can add ice.

Muli Parantha

- First time and hope it is not the last.
- Different than other paranthas.

Dal Puri

- Something new that I've never eaten before. Goes well with everything. Love the story behind it.

Ladoos

- Reminds me of Mathura Ladoos. Nice touch with the crispy stuff like coconut.
- Very good. Just enough sweetness to end a meal, and with a hint of coconut.
- Seems too much work, store ones are sweeter though.

Nan Khatai

- Nice and crispy, like a cookie.

Quinoa Kheer

- Healthy and a good dessert.
- Good, but the flavor is very pronounced. I wouldn't eat a whole bowl on it's own.
- Different than usual, but good.
- A nice, light dessert.

Muttar Paneer

- Love the tanginess and a little taste of amchur.
- Very tasty!
- Muttar Paneer is great and very familiar.
- Muttar Paneer is my favorite dish. I love the crunch of the green peas and the cubes of paneer.

KITCHEN ADVICE

We watched a senior in her late 70's offer a plate of kadhi as a sample to a volunteer writing the recipe, then offer the same plate to her mother in (her early 90's); we then came to know that this very kadhi had been passed down by her grandmother through generations. The volunteer knew that the 90-year-old mother had already eaten her lunch and nevertheless asked the elder mother if she cared to join in sampling the food. Without hesitation, and with a big smile, she took the plate, put it on her lap, and began to indulge as she told her stories. The daughter was overjoyed, and whispered to the Aangan volunteer that it was not the food but the love and company that has given her mother this joy; we realized how happy it made her feel just by our visiting her. We learned the when her mother was younger and new to Canada, she could not speak a word of English or French. Even as she aged, she would take public transportation and stand close to the bus driver gesturing by pointing her finger to a piece of paper to indicate where she needed to get off. We admire her strength and independent spirit!

Kitchen Advice

• **Cleaning burnt food from a pan:** Add a drop or two of dish soap and enough water to cover the bottom of the pan. Bring the water to boil and it cleans the pan easily.

• **Celery:** Wrap the celery in an aluminum foil before putting it in the refrigerator. It will keep it fresh for weeks!

• **Corn on the Cob:** Add a pinch of sugar to help bring out the corn's natural taste.

•**Cleaning a Thermos Bottle:** Fill the bottle with water. Drop in four Alka Seltzer tablets and let it soak for 1 hour (or longer if necessary).

•**Burn Curing:** It's very interesting to see notice seniors keeping some flour in a container in the freezer. They do so to use it if they get burnt. Keep the burnt part in flour for 10 minutes and no blister will form. It also lessens the burning sensation. Room temperature and white flour could be used for this purpose, however cold flour sooths the pain faster. Some apply a bit of ghee to soothe a burn.

•**Bean Sprouts:** Put sprouts in a container of cold water and refrigerate to keep them crisp for 4 days.

•**Cleaning a Manual Can-Opener:** To clean a manual can-opener, run a folded sheet of paper towel through it. The paper towel helps clean the gear and the blade of the opener.

•**Papadams and stale chips**: Microwave papadam in oven at high setting for 2 minutes. Restore stale potato and tortilla chips by spreading in plate, set on high and microwave for 1 minute. Place on paper towel to cool to room temperature and serve.

•**Oil spills on the floor:** If oil spills on the floor, sprinkle with a thick layer of flour or dry mud or sand and wait a few minutes for the flour to soak up the oil. Then wipe the area with paper towel. Spray with window cleaner and you will have no trace of oil on the floor.

•**Tea Stains on Ceramic:** Tea stains build up due to tea in mugs. These are easily removed by taking a cut lemon dipped in coarse salt (to act as an abrasive agent if need to scrub away the stains) and using it to wash the mug in hot soapy water.

•**To clean stained teapots/tea cups**, drop a denture cleaning tablet (i.e. polident). Soak for a few hours, wash pot or cup in hot water and repeat if stains are old and too deep.

Did You Know?

- **A sealed Envelope:** Freeze for 2- 3 hours, open the flap with the knife. This way the envelope can be resealed again.

- **Empty toilet paper:** Can be used as a appliance cord holder. You can label it and store it neatly.

- **Icy door step:** Put Dawn liquid dish washing soap in warm water and pour it on the door steps, they will not refreeze, for a considerable number of days!

- **Old wax glass candle:** Put the old glass candle in the freezer for few hours, and turn it upside down after taking it out of the freezer. It will fall off easily.

- **S.O.S pads:** Cut them in half as it is more economical and will last indefinitely. This way it sharpens the scissors as well.

- **Blood stains on Clothes:** Pour some hydrogen peroxide on a cloth and rub it on the blood stains to wipe them off.

- **Washing Windows:** Use vertical strokes outside and horizontal strokes inside. This way you can tell which side has the streaks. Using vinegar will get the windows outside very clean. Do not wash windows on a sunny day, because they will dry too quickly to form streaks.

- **Scented Light:** Simply spray your favorite perfume on the light bulb and create a lovely lit scented room.

- **Fresh smelling clothes:** Place fabric softener sheets in the dresser drawers. This way your clothes will smell fresh for the weeks to come.

- **Candles**: They will last long if placed in the freezer for 3 hours prior to burning.

- **Artificial flower cleaning:** Pour some salt into a paper bag with the artificial flower in it. Shake it rigorously; as the salt absorbs all the dust and dirt, your artificial flower will remain looking new. Works like a charm!

- **Clean Burnt Food on the pan:** Add a drop or two of dish soap and enough water to cover the bottom of the pan. Bring the water to boil and clean easily.

- **Celery:** Wrap the celery in an aluminium foil before putting it in the refrigerator. It will keep it fresh for weeks!

- **Corn on the Cob:** Add a pinch of sugar to help bring out the corn's natural taste.

- **Splinter:** Before going for a needle or tweezers, try scotch tape surface to pull out the splinter. It makes it easier and less painful.

- **Clean Thermos Bottle:** Fill the bottle with water. Drop in four Alka Seltzer tablets and let it soak for 1 hour (or longer if necessary).

Benefits of Spices and Herbs

Anardana

(*Pomegranate seeds*) It's a native of Iran and has a sour taste, hence its wide use. It contains vitamin A and C and aids in digestion. It soothes headaches, acidity and flatulence.

Asafoetida

(*Hing*) It is a distinctive and pungent spice found in powdered form. When cooked, it has a roasted garlic aroma. Used in cooking of beans and lentils for it's digestive and anti-flatulence properties. Pinch of it can be fried in hot oil before the rest of the ingredients are cooked.

Bay Leaf

Contains compounds called parthenolides that are helpful for treatment of migraines. Contains eugenol with anti-inflammatory and ani-oxidant properties, so used in herbal cold-remedies.

Black pepper

"King of spice". Is anti-inflammatory, anti-flatulent and contains antioxidant vitamins A and C. It is disease-preventing and health-promoting. It is native to the western ghats of the Kerala state from where it has spread to the rest of the world.

Cardamom (black)

Known as the hill cardamom. Comes from Nepal. Used to treat stomach disorders and malaria. It is the main ingredient in garam masala. Helps to detoxify the body and helps prevent urinary tract infections, soothes muscle pain and promotes healthy appetites. Combats oral infections.

Cardamom (green)

Versatile spice used in Indian curries, desserts and teas. Counteracts stomach acidity, stimulates appetite, ease nausea, cures bad breath and relieves gas and bloating. Contains antioxidants and is used as an aphrodisiac and to fight obesity.

Ajwain

(*Carom Seed*) Close to oregano. Has antibacterial and anti-inflammatory effects, caraway has been used for cold relief, toothaches and to boost immune function. It also aids digestion, settles stomach and relieves bloating. It is had by boiling 4 glasses of water with 2 tablespoons of ajwain. Cool and drink throughout the day.

Chilli Powder

Cayenne peppers' bright red color signals its high content of beta-carotene or pro-vitamin A. It includes both the ground seeds as well as the dried flesh. By providing heat in the dish one may perspire and cool down the body. Hence, this is widely used in hot climate areas.

Cloves

Anti-bacterial and anti-fungal properties. Also aids in detoxification from environmental pollutants. Helps relieves the pain of toothache.

Coriander seeds

Seeds of cilantro plant. Contains antioxidants to help animal fats from becoming rancid and has anti-bacterial qualities. It soothes the stomach and relieves bloating. It is oil remedy for arthritis relief.

Cumin

Is a diuretic (helps the body shed water), relieve diarrhea and bowel spasms, morning sickness and eases carpal tunnel syndrome.

Kala Jeera

(*Black Cumin*) Folklore says it's a cure-all maybe because for auto-immune disorders it's a good natural remedy. It restores harmony as it cures upset stomachs, headaches, toothaches, colds and infections. Very dramatic in healing asthma and allergies. Middle-easterners use it to treat bronchitis.

Methi

(*Fenugreek seeds*) Anti-inflammatory properties and aids digestion. Helps reduce blood sugar levels when used with insulin. It is an expectorant and used for easing congestion, allergies and bronchitis.

Kalanji

(*Onion seeds*) Useful for removing parasitic worms. Soothes headaches, toothaches and allergies. Has fever reducing properties and increases respiration.

Ginger

Used to naturally treat nausea from morning and motion sickness. Has anti-inflamatory properties to help ease muscle and joint pain. It also causes sweating and is used to detoxify the body, stimulate circulation, ease bronchitis and congestion. Added in many foods and Indian tea.

Kala namak

(*Black Salt*) High in iron. Has no sodium so good for high blood-pressure patients and people on low-sodium diets. Has a very sulfuric aroma which displeases the nose, so is generally avoided.

Amchur

(*Mango powder*) Rich source of vitamin A, E and selenium which help protect from heart disease. Has antioxidant and anti-cancer properties. It is high in iron, combats acidity and is effective in unclogging pores of skin.

Rai

(*Mustard seeds*) Is anti-inflammatory, soothes asthma and rhematoid artritis. It's a source of magnesium and lowers high blood pressure. Helps people with lack of appetite when take 15 minutes before meal.

Paprika

Has anti-inflammatory and antioxidant properties as it contains capsicum.

Poppy seeds

Have antioxidants and lower bad cholesterol. These help prevent heart disease and strokes by helping to maintain a healthy blood-lipid profile. These seeds are a source of B-complex vitamins.

Turmeric

"Queen of spices". Found in most curries. Has antioxidants needed for liver detox and has anti-inflammatory effects so used for arthritic pains. Fights fat belly inhibits growth of fat cells. Many of our seniors take 1/2 teaspoon of it in warm milk or water daily. It is applied by on fresh cuts to heal wounds and stop blood flow.

Cilantro

Commonly known as "hara dhaniya" or green coriander. The green leaves contain protein, fat, minerals, vitamins, fiber, carbohydrates and water. Vitamin C, calcium, phosphorus, iron carotene and oxalic acid. It helps strengthen stomach and promotes digestion.

Cinnamon

Like cardamom, it's pleasant aroma stimulates the senses yet calms the nerves. Stimulates blood flow and is helpful for weight loss.

Kari putha or Neem

(*Curry Leaves*)Useful for good hair, improved function of the small intestine and soothing kidney pains. Soothe skin infections and heat rash. Great for treating acne, certain eye disorders and lowering bad cholesterol levels and morning sickness. They contain iron, calcium, Vitamin C, phosphorous and fiber.

Methi leaves

(*Fenugreek leaves*) These are cooling and mildly laxative and enriched with vitamin C and K. It has fiber and can help lower bad cholesterol and lower chances of type 1 and 2 diabetes.

Garam Masala

In hindi it means "hot" (garam) mixture of spices (masala). Full of flavor and made from cloves cardamom, cumin, peppercorns, cinnamon and bay leaves.

Garlic

Has antibacterial, anti-viral and anti-fungal properties. May prevent high cholesterol, high blood pressure, cancer and helps regulate blood sugar levels.

Nutmeg

A good source of copper, potassium, calcium, iron, zinc and many VHAL B-complex vitamins. It is anti-fungal, an anti-depressant and has antioxidants like beta carotene.

Saffron

Most expensive spice. May treat depression, asthma, mentrual pains and may have anti-cancer effects. It also helps lower cholesterol.

Tamarind

Native of Sudan and introduced into India centuries ago. It has antiseptic, mild laxative and digestive properties. Excellent to polish copper and brass items as well. Its tangy flavor makes a popular replacement for lemon in South Indian cooking as it grows widely there.

Glossary

A

Arhar Dal	Split Red Gram
Adrak	Ginger
Ajwain	Carom Seeds / Thyme
Amchur	Dried Mango Powder
Anar Dana	Pomegranate Seeds (Dried)
Atta	Wheat Flour
Andaza	To estimate
Achar	Pickle
Alu	Potato
Akhrot	Walnut

B

Baghar	Spices and herbs are added one at a time to hot oil, known as tempering. Also known as tadka or chonk.
Bhunao	A browning process involving stirring till the oil separates from the masala. Slow cooking and low heat yield best results.
Bhunna	Roasted
Bhigohna	To Soak
Badam	Almond
Besan	Gram Flour
Bhutta	Corn Cobs
Black Cumin Seeds	Caraway Seeds

C

Chana	Bengal Gram & Chickpeas (brown)
Chawli	Black Eyed Beans
Chane Ka Atta	Gram Flour
Chawal	Rice
Chana Dal	Split Bengal Gram
Chhuara	Dates (Dried)
Chiwda	Flaked, Beaten rice
Chonk	See Baghar
Chillah	Besan pancakes
Chune	Slaked lime
Chilgoza	Pine nut
Chakriphool	Star Anise

D

Dhuanaar	Smoked. Ghee is poured on hot coals and covered with the meat to give smoked flavor
Do-Piaza	Named after Mullah Do-Piaza, who could apparently cook delights using only two onions. 'Do' for two and 'piaza' for onions.
Dum	To steam. In the olden days, the heavy vessel was sealed with atta (dough) to capture all the moisture within the food being slowly cooked.
Dalia	Broken Wheat

Dahi	Curd
Dalchini	Cinnamon
Dhania Patta	Coriander Leaves
Dhania Powder	Coriander Powder
Dhakna	To cover
Dudh	Milk

E

Elaichi (Chhoti)	Green Cardamom or Chotti Elaichi
Elaichi (Moti)	Brown Cardamom or Kali Elaichi

G

Gehun	Wheat
Gehun Ka Atta	Wheat Flour
Ghee	Clarified Butter
Gulab Pani	Rose Water

H

Handi	Vessel. Bhunao and dum are best in a thick bottom handi
Hara Chana	Chickpeas (green)
Hari Mirch	Green Chilly
Hing	Asafoetida

I

Imli	Tamarind
Ittar	Vertivier, perfume

J

Jaiphal	Nutmeg
Javitri	Mace
Jeera	Cumin Seed

K

Kadhai	Round bottom wide open heavy pan, like a wok.
Kali Dal	Black Gram or Sabut
Kabuli Chana	Chickpeas (white)
Kaali Dal	Split Black Gram
Kaju	Cashew Nut
Kala Jeera	Black cumin seeds or Shahi Jeera
Kala Namak	Rock Salt
Kali Mirch	Black Pepper
Kari Patta	Curry Leaves
Kheera	Cucumber
Khoya	Fresh Dried Whole Milk or Thickened Milk
Kishmish	Raisins
Kurmura	Puffed Rice
Kalonji	Black Onion Seeds
Kewda	Vetivier
Khajur	Dates
Kasoori Methi	FTenugreek
Khus Khus	Poppy Seeds
Kesar	Saffron

L

Lobhia	Black Eyed Beans
Lahsun	Garlic or Lasan
Laung	Clove

M

Moong	Green Gram
Makai Ka Atta	Maize Flour
Masoor	Red Lentil
Maida	White Flour
Moong Dal	Split Green Gram
Masoor Dal	Split Red Lentil
Malai	The portion of cream that rises to the top after milk has boiled and cooled
Mattha (Chhaach)	Butter Milk
Methi	Fenugreek Seeds
Mirch	Chilli
Moong Fali	Groundnut
Magaz	Melon Seeds
Munakka	Sultana

N

Nimboo ka Sat	Citric Acid
Nimboo	Lime, also spelt Nimbu or Neeboo

O

Okhali	Pestle and motor.

P

Poha	Flaked, Beaten rice
Paneer	Indian cheese from boiled fresh milk
Patta Gobi	Cabbage
Pao	Bun or spelt 'Pau'
Phitkari	Alum
Phool Gobi	Cauliflower
Pudina	Mint
Phatna	To whip or beat

R

Rajma	Red Kidney Beans
Rava	Semolina
Rai	Small Mustard Seeds

S

Suji	Semolina
Sonth	Dry Ginger Powder
Saboodana	Sago, also spelled Sabudana
Sarson	Fresh Green Mustard
Saunf	Fennel or Aniseed
Shimla Mirch	Green Capsicum
Sukha Podina	Dried Mint
Sukha Narial	Desiccated Coconut

Sukhana	To dry
Sabut	Whole

T

Talna	To fry
Tawa	Flat Round heavy pan, used to make rotis.
Tuvar Dal	Split Red Gram
Tadka	See baghar
Tej Patta	Bay Leaf
Til	Sesame seeds, Kala-til (Black sesame)
Tulsi	Indian Basil

U

Urad Dal	Black Lentil Sabut, Split Black Lentil and Washed White Split Lentil

V

Varq	Silver Leaves

Made in the USA
Charleston, SC
31 August 2012